PERSONAL FOUL

PERSONAL FOUL

Coach Joe Moore vs. The University of Notre Dame

———————————

RICHARD LIEBERMAN

Published in 2001 by
Academy Chicago Publishers
363 West Erie Street
Chicago, Illinois 60610

Library of Congress Cataloging-in-Publication Data

Lieberman, Richard (Richard E.)
    Personal foul : Coach Joe Moore vs. the University of Notre
    Dame / Richard Lieberman.
        p. cm.
    Includes index.
    ISBN 0-89733-489-2
    1. Moore, Joe, 1932?—Trials, litigation, etc. 2. University of
Notre Dame—Trials, litigation, etc. 3. Age discrimination in
employment—Law and legislation—Indiana. 4. College sports—
Moral and ethical aspects—Indiana—South Bend. I. Title.

    KF228.M64 L54 2001
    796.332'63'0977289—dc21
                                            00-050257

"Tis known by the name of perseverance in a good cause,—and of obstinacy in a bad one."

LAURENCE STERNE
TRISTRAM SHANDY

"Cheer, cheer for old Notre Dame."

NOTRE DAME FIGHT SONG

CONTENTS

I

———

DECEMBER 1996:
SOUTH BEND & CHICAGO

Early on a grey December morning, while he was getting dressed, Joe Moore received an unexpected telephone call. His new boss, Bob Davie, wanted to drop by and see him for a minute. Joe told his wife Fran, who quickly began straightening the living room. Frowning at the blaring television set, Joe pulled on an old grey sweatshirt. He and Fran had weathered faces, iron grey hair and sturdy physiques reflecting years of physical labor. They lived in a modest apartment across the street from the university campus in South Bend, Indiana.

When the bell rang a few minutes later, Joe opened the door to Davie, a tall, well-groomed blond man in his forties, wearing sharply pressed slacks and a blue sport jacket over his shirt and tie. The two men sat on the couch, and Fran excused herself, walking around the corner into the small hall leading to the master bedroom. Halfway there, she stopped to listen.

She heard Davie say, after asking her husband to lower the volume on the television set, "Joe, this is the hardest thing I've ever had to do in my life. I've known you for twenty years." He went on to say that he had just signed a five-year contract with the university, and believed that Joe could continue working for only one, or possibly two, more years. He needed someone, he said, for the full five years.

In his gravelly voice, her husband protested that he was planning on working at least three or four more years, and would see how he felt after that.

Davie cut him off. "At your age," he said flatly, "I can't count on you for five more years. I need somebody younger."

Fran could not listen any longer. She walked into the bedroom and sat on the bed, weeping. Several minutes later, Joe came into the room and stood looking down at her. When he was defeated, he resembled a sad basset hound, an expression that never failed to provoke her deepest protective instincts. As he stood silent, she willed herself to stop crying. In a steely voice, she said, "He can't do that!"

He shook his head. "What do you mean he can't do that?"

"He can't do that. It's age discrimination."

"You're crazy," he said, smiling sadly. "He's the coach of Notre Dame. He can fire anybody he wants."

Joe Moore was the offensive line coach for the most famous football team in the world. For nine years, in partnership with the head coach, Lou Holtz, he led the team into the nation's top twenty college football team rankings every year but one. Once, they won a national championship; twice they ranked second in the country and in other years, they ranked in fourth and sixth place. Joe Moore coached the crown jewel of the Notre Dame football team—the offensive line: the seven players who protect the player moving the ball forward on the field. Sports commentators considered Notre Dame's offensive line the best in college football, and Joe Moore the premier offensive line coach in the entire football profession. But on the morning of December 2, 1996, he had become merely an unemployed, sixty-four-year-old man.

That evening, a local South Bend businessman and friend of the Moores stopped by. Earlier in the day, he had heard from a player's father that Bob Davie, the new head coach, had announced to the offensive line players that Coach Moore had decided to retire.

Joe, still in shock, was suddenly angry. "I recruited every one of them kids to come to Notre Dame and play under me," he said in his foghorn voice. "I promised them I would be their coach during the entire time they were here. For Davie to tell those kids that I retired is the same as saying I welshed on my commitment to them. He said I retired because he didn't have the guts to say he fired me!"

That night, sleepless in the dark, he became more and more incensed over what Davie had done to him. The bitter irony was that he himself was responsible for bringing Davie to Notre Dame's coaching staff, and as a result, Davie had just received one of the most coveted jobs in America. Three years before, when Notre Dame needed a new defensive coordinator, Joe had strongly recommended that Lou Holtz hire Davie, then the thirty-nine-year-old defensive coordinator at Texas A&M. In the 1980s, Joe and Davie had coached together for several years at the University of Pittsburgh, and Joe felt Davie was an up-and-comer in the college football coaching ranks. Despite Joe's recommendation, Holtz had hesitated to hire Davie: he had never heard of him, and he didn't like Davie's coaching at Texas A&M, a school that had repeatedly violated NCAA rules. But Joe urged Holtz at least to interview Davie, and Holtz finally relented. But when Joe approached him, Davie said that he did not want to work under Holtz because Holtz had a reputation of being tough on assistant coaches. Joe pressed Davie to meet with Holtz, telling him that "an assistant coaching job at Notre Dame is the best stepping-stone to a head coaching job at a first-tier college football program," and that if Davie really wanted to be a head coach, his prospects were far better as assistant coach at Notre Dame than at Texas A &M.

Davie took Joe's advice and, in early 1994, became Notre Dame's defensive coordinator. Davie immediately attached himself to Joe, relying on him as a friend and mentor. Almost every day he stopped at Joe's office, down the hall from his own, to gossip, discuss football, and seek career advice. As time passed, Davie's desire for a head coaching job increased, and he plotted his strategy while Joe listened and offered suggestions. Joe didn't think that Davie needed any help in the art of political maneuvering. Davie was a master of the game; he knew who to court and who to ignore. Holtz's relationship with the new athletic director, Michael Wadsworth, was strained and there was a possibility that Holtz might resign, opening up the head coaching job. Even if that was only a remote possibility, Davie carefully cultivated relationships with Wadsworth and anyone else he thought could help him. Joe believed that Davie, with his movie star looks and natural ease with the media, was indeed a prime candidate for any top tier head coaching job—even at Notre Dame.

During the 1995 season, when Holtz had minor surgery and missed several games, Davie filled in for him. Before his first game as acting head coach against Vanderbilt, Davie addressed the team, saying, "Even though we're playing without Coach Holtz, we'll win because we've got Coach Moore with his tremendous experience and ability." At several difficult points during the game, Davie walked over to Joe and asked him what plays he thought they should run. Notre Dame decisively beat Vanderbilt, and Davie, ecstatic, hugged Moore at the post-game celebration.

The night of his firing, Joe lay in bed, his mind endlessly replaying the day's events. He thought how completely mistaken he had been to believe, when Holtz announced his resignation a few weeks before, and Davie was appointed his successor, that he himself would coach at least another five years at Notre Dame.

The next day Joe went to the football office to confront Davie, but he was not there. Unable to conceal his frustration, Joe told the secretaries that he was looking for Davie. The following day Joe went looking for him again; this time, he saw him coming down the hallway and asked him into his private office. Once inside, Joe unleashed his anger and frustration. "On Monday morning you fire me," Joe rasped. "Then on Monday afternoon you meet with my offensive linemen and tell them that I retired or resigned."

"I did it for your benefit," Davie replied calmly.

"My benefit! You didn't do it for my benefit, you did it for your benefit! You were afraid to tell them you fired me. You were afraid you wouldn't look good."

"What do you want me to do?"

"All I want is the truth, no more. Just the truth. I am not retiring." Joe lowered his voice in an effort to control himself. "I don't have any money. How'm I going to retire? I have to work. And I promised those kids I wouldn't leave them, and then you go ahead and tell them that I retired." He began to get worked up again. "I want you to tell the truth! Just tell the truth!"

Davie did not lose his composure. He slowly stood up, hesitating for a moment as if he was carefully weighing his words. Finally, in a flat voice, he said, "Fuck you," turned, and walked out of the room. Staring at the empty chair, Joe bitterly muttered, "Fuck you too." For the first time in his adult life, he was at a complete loss about what to do next. He sat for awhile and then went home.

At my office in the Ross & Hardies law firm, I glanced through a stack of phone messages that had accumulated during the morning while I was on a conference call. I saw three "urgent" messages from my partner Rick Mason, but I had to call a client first. The paging system kept repeating Rick's extension number, but I always put the client's requirements first, so I wasn't able to respond right away.

It was an overcast December morning, and as I looked out the wide window at the grey expanse of Lake Michigan, I felt rather depressed. I had just turned fifty, and although I still felt (and I hope looked) younger than my age, I was beginning to feel the lack of a challenge: it seemed to me that I had essentially achieved everything I had hoped to in my career.

The paging system continued to signal me, but I was still tied up. Finally, Rick Mason and another partner, Tim Klenk, came into my office. After I hung up, Rick explained that he and Tim had discussed a call Rick had received from a friend who had been in his class at Notre Dame Law School. This friend told Rick that Notre Dame had just fired their star offensive line coach, Joe Moore, and a number of alumni were encouraging Moore to talk to a labor lawyer to find out whether his firing had violated any laws. His friend asked Rick to arrange a consultation for the coach with an expert in employment law.

Tim said that he had reminded Rick that it was department policy to represent only corporate clients; since I was head of the labor and employment group, they had to talk to me about it, although they knew I strongly supported this policy. Ross & Hardies lawyers billed these clients up to $300 an hour. If we were to represent individuals on employment matters, we would probably have to do it on a contingency basis with payment depending on whether we won the case. And if we were to represent individuals, we might find ourselves suing—and alienating—potential corporate clients. Apart from the money, it seemed to us to be philosophically inconsistent to represent parties on both sides of the fence in employment and labor cases.

Taking all this into consideration, Tim had already suggested to Rick that Moore be referred to a capable plaintiff's employment firm in Chicago. The only question was choosing the best firm for the coach.

I wasn't a sports fan, and I didn't know anything about Notre Dame's offensive line coach—I didn't even know the name of the head coach. But I did know that Notre Dame's was the most prominent football team in the world; that Knute Rockne had coached at Notre Dame and the Gipper, a Notre Dame football player, had been played by Ronald Reagan in the movies. I even remembered listening, when I was in college, to a radio broadcast of Notre Dame playing Michigan State for the national football championship some time in the mid-1960s when Ara Parseghian was coach.

I asked Rick why Moore wanted to meet with us.

"Possible age discrimination," Rick said. "Apparently someone talked about his age when he was fired."

"They actually mentioned his age in connection with his firing?" I asked. I found that incredible.

That, Rick said, was what had upset Moore.

Against my better judgment, I said, "Why don't we at least talk to this guy?"

This surprised Tim; he decided I was merely being polite, and that we would give Moore advice and refer the case to another firm.

The following day, Joe and his wife Fran were on Interstate 80, driving ninety miles to Chicago through the gently rolling farmland of northern Indiana. During the drive, they talked about whether they could possibly pay for a lawsuit. Their life savings amounted to only $25,000. If the lawyers thought there was a case, Joe was willing to spend their entire nest egg, but Fran told him, "Joe, Chicago law firms can charge $25,000 a month for a lawsuit."

"Fran, I'd spend every penny we have on a lawsuit against them for just one month. That's how I feel."

Throughout the thirty-eight years of their married life, Fran had been his partner and advisor. They had met on a blind date in May, 1955, when she was a student at Montefiore Hospital School of Nursing in Pittsburgh, and Joe was a star football player at Penn State. Fran was a very determined and focused young woman whose father, chief of police in her Pennsylvania hometown of Rankin, was her role model. She had been a leader and valedictorian in high school and nursing college.

On this first date, Joe took her to a cabaret in downtown Pittsburgh where performers imitated Judy Garland, Marlene Dietrich and other popular singers of the day. As they sat in the dark club, Fran thought it was incongruous that a rough and tough football player would choose such sophisticated entertainment. As she watched, she was struck suddenly by the singer's sturdy legs, broad shoulders and deep voice. "If I didn't know better," she whispered to Joe, "I'd say that that woman is a man." Joe shrugged and chuckled. Fran asked him what was so funny. He hesitated, and she persisted. Finally, he said, "She *is* a man. They're all men in dresses." Fran had heard of female impersonator bars, but she never thought that someone would take her to one on a first date. This guy's a nut, she thought. But he's cute and funny.

Later in the evening he took her to a crowded neighborhood bar. Sitting at a table in the back of the noisy, smoke-filled room, Joe told her that he had just reentered college after almost two years in the service. His family lived in Pittsburgh and his father, John Lawrence "Dinty" Moore, whom Joe spoke of with great admiration, had been a legendary local Pittsburgh baseball and football player. After Dinty Moore's playing days ended, he managed sandlot baseball teams. "When Honus Wagner, the great baseball player, retired from the majors, he played for my dad's team," Joe proudly told her. "I was the bat boy for my Dad's team and met Wagner."

In his deep, gravelly voice, Joe told Fran that, like his father, he had played football and baseball in high school. He got about fifty offers from colleges to play football and accepted a scholarship with the University of Tennessee. He was the freshman quarterback, but the adjustment to southern Tennessee was difficult for a boy born and bred in an eastern steel town surrounded by family. After his freshman year, he transferred to Penn State. But he struggled at Penn, earning only about thirteen credit hours in two years. When he flunked ROTC, he decided that college was not for him. But twenty-one months in the army changed his opinion about college, and after the service, he returned to Penn State and focused on his studies, getting good grades. As the starting running back for Penn State, he realized that he loved the game of football more than anything, except his family. He also greatly admired his coaches at Penn, and told Fran that, if things worked out, he would like to be a football coach himself.

After only three dates, Fran accepted his fraternity pin, and at Christmas he took her home to meet his family. Fran was struck by the family's devout Catholicism. All three of his aunts on his father's side were nuns. Joe's father never left the house without crossing himself. Fran thought the whole family was wonderful and unique. Joe and his three brothers had the same distinctive voice—like a foghorn with a Pittsburgh accent. When Fran phoned the Moore house, she could never tell if it was Joe or one of his three brothers (he had one sister) who was answering.

They were married three-and-a-half years later. Joe's first job was as a graduate assistant under Coach Joe Paterno at Penn State, and what he learned from Paterno served as the basis of his coaching technique for the rest of his career. In 1959, Joe and Fran moved to Richfield Springs, New York, where Joe taught history at the high school and was head coach of the school's football and baseball teams. By the second year, his exceptional talent as a football coach became apparent when his team won the division championship. The following year Fran and Joe returned to Pennsylvania, and over the next fifteen years he taught and coached football at three high schools, where he compiled an extraordinary overall record of 118-30-2 and won six league titles. During those years, they raised their three sons.

By the time Joe reached his mid-forties, he and Fran assumed he would spend the rest of his career as a high school coach and teacher. But in 1976, the University of Pittsburgh hired a new head coach, Jackie Sherill, who wanted a local high school coach on his staff. Joe was Sherill's obvious choice. As always, Fran was the co-decision maker. She and Joe weighed the pros and cons of taking the job. College coaching positions can be extremely unstable: if the head coach leaves, his assistants might not be retained. The Moores did not want to move from job to job every few years. On the other hand, the combined pressure of teaching history, coaching and dealing with the administrative and parent-relations aspects of his high school job, was beginning to wear on Joe. At Pitt, he would be able to concentrate solely on coaching, and ultimately that was the deciding factor.

As it worked out, the Moores did not have to worry about job security. Joe spent nine years at Pitt: three years as the offensive backfield coach and six years as the offensive line coach. When Sherill left, his successor Foge Fazio did not hesitate to retain Joe.

After nine years at Pitt, Joe moved to Temple University. When he had been at Temple for two years, Joe's old boss from Pittsburgh, Jackie Sherill, was contacted by Notre Dame's head coach Lou Holtz who was putting a first-class coaching staff together.

Holtz had been hired by Notre Dame two years before, in 1986, with a mandate to restore the football program to national prominence. While Notre Dame had a glorious history, with Rockne, Gipp, the Four Horsemen and the highest winning percentage of all college football teams, by 1986 the program had fallen on hard times. During the preceding five years, the team had performed miserably under Coach Gerry Faust, never even finishing in the top twenty rankings. Holtz, intense and articulate, was under immense pressure to turn things around quickly. But during his first two seasons, the team continued to perform poorly, losing six out of eleven games in 1986 and improving only slightly to a eight-and-four record in 1987.

In that second season, Holtz called Jackie Sherill, who was then coaching at Texas A&M, and asked for his recommendations for assistant coaches. Sherill did not hesitate to tell Holtz that Joe Moore was the best assistant coach in

college football: "He can coach offense, defense, the line—
you name it. If you have a chance to hire him, do it."

When Holtz invited Joe to South Bend for an interview,
Joe and Fran were delighted. Joe thought about how his late
father would have reacted: Dinty Moore had considered
Notre Dame the *ne plus ultra* of college football as well as of
Catholic education. To add to Joe's pleasure, several of his
friends told him that they had heard that Holtz was prepared to hire him on the spot.

The two men met in Holtz's office on the edge of the
1,300 acre campus. In most respects, Notre Dame looks like
any other traditional college campus with its broad green
quadrangles and brick buildings, old and new. What is distinctive about this campus is the immense golden dome on
the administration building. This dome dominates the campus, giving it an ethereal, almost other-worldly look. Almost
as striking is the massive football stadium, one half mile in
circumference and forty-five feet high, built in 1929, during
the Rockne era. Until fairly recently, fans entering the stadium encountered the startling spectacle of a giant mosaic
of Jesus Christ which covered the side of the adjacent library
building, and loomed over one of the end zones.

The interview with Holtz did not go well. Coaches whom
Joe had worked under at Temple and Pitt were generally not
interested in coaching fundamentals, preferring to leave details to the assistant coaches. Joe appreciated that approach
because he had very definite ideas about football fundamentals. Joe worked constantly to teach his kids to master basics
like the proper way for a player to aim his pads and to place
his feet and hands. If a player had difficulty keeping his pads

aimed low, Joe made him write, "I will keep my pads low. I will keep my pads low. I will keep my pads low," over and over again until the young man internalized the skill. To Joe's surprise, Holtz began passionately discussing his own notion of fundamental techniques.

Joe strongly disagreed with much of what Holtz was saying, and, against his better judgment, began to argue with him. The two men disputed the proper approach for the "double team"—where two players block a single player. Holtz maintained that one player should go for the legs and the other should attack the upper body. Joe believed that both players should use the same precisely structured and executed blocking technique. Joe told Holtz that he realized that many coaches disagreed with his highly technical approach; rather, they preferred Holtz's approach to the "double team." But to Joe, nothing was more important than mastering perfect technique. With correct technique, a team can control the line of scrimmage so that even average athletes can win fifty percent of the time, and with top athletes, a team can win almost all the time. To teach technique, Joe told Holtz, he believed in repetition. "The kids learn that there is no easy way to do anything; without inner strength, it's all wrong, and with inner strength it's right," he said.

Holtz was willing to work with a man whose strong will matched his own; he told Joe they would be open to using his techniques. But he warned him: "If they don't work, we'll change it to my way."

They never changed it.

Joe's first season at Notre Dame passed in a surrealistic blur. Since the team was not as strong as many of its competitors, and its starting quarterback had been benched the previous season for poor performance, Joe had only modest expectations. But the team won game after game, and when it was all over, Notre Dame was the national champion with a 12-0 record. In one season, Notre Dame had become Notre Dame once again.

Over the next eight years, Joe's offensive line was the heart of Notre Dame football. Almost every year, rushing statistics—the number of yards gained by that offensive line— ranked in the top ten of the nation's college football teams. As Joe told a reporter, "When the offensive line plays well, the running backs look good. When the running backs look good, the quarterback and receivers look good." Any knowledgeable football fan understood perfectly well what Joe meant—a team's success rises and falls on the performance of the offensive line.

Every year in December, Notre Dame holds a football banquet honoring its players. In 1993, after presenting the Notre Dame monogram to the star players and listening to Regis Philbin speak reverently of the accomplishments of the team, still in contention for that year's national title, Joe was called to the podium and named an honorary member of the Notre Dame Monogram Club—the highest football honor the university could bestow.

Caught entirely off guard, Joe wept as he stood before the audience of 2,000. "In times like these, I think of my father and what he would have said," he rumbled, barely audibly. "He would have cried, and that's what I'm doing."

The Moores met with Tim Klenk, Rick Mason and me— in our 27th floor conference room. Moore didn't look like my stereotyped idea of a big-time football coach. I had ex-

pected someone burly and overbearing. Joe Moore, at about
five feet ten and 165 pounds, seemed, if anything, small and
deferential. What was not surprising was that, like most employees who had just been fired, he appeared to be in shock.
I had handled hundreds of termination cases for corporate
clients, and had often noticed this. Losing a job, even in the
most benign way, can cause almost the same reaction as losing a spouse. If one's essential identity is linked with one's
occupation, this abrupt termination can be psychologically
devastating.

As Moore told his story, it was obvious that his entire
identity was linked to Notre Dame. Coaching there, he told
us, was "the job of a lifetime, a dream come true": Notre
Dame's tradition, its great kids, its high academic standards,
its demanding schedule with every game on network television—to say nothing of the extraordinary people he was able
to meet. He had the second-best football coaching job in the
country; the best was, of course, Notre Dame's head coach.
To Joe, Notre Dame was a kind of Catholic Disneyland. He
told us that his grandchildren loved to spend the entire summer in South Bend with him and Fran. John Patrick, their
oldest grandchild, had visited every summer during the nine
years they lived in South Bend, and Christopher, a younger
grandchild, had begun spending the summer when he reached
the age of five.

As Moore talked slowly and deliberately in his low, hoarse
voice, his high intelligence was apparent. He expressed himself clearly and cogently, and demonstrated an excellent
memory for details. It occurred to me that a great coach
must be a great teacher. Moore described the firing, mentioning that Davie had told him that he would receive eigh-

teen months' severance pay until he turned sixty-five. Davie seemed to think that Moore was going to be sixty-five in a year and a half. When Moore told him that he would be sixty-five in only two months, Davie said that he would check into it. At this point, a week after the termination, no one had gotten back to Joe on his severance pay. He planned to look for another job, but was not sure about his prospects, particularly since Notre Dame considered him too old to coach and had announced that he had retired.

It seemed to me that the suddenness of the firing and Davie's pronouncement that he was too old to coach had had a traumatic effect on Moore. He had come to our office, I thought, not so much because he had made a dispassionate decision to pursue his legal rights, but because he had suffered a debilitating personal loss and did not know where to turn.

Moore said his health was good, and there was no reason why he couldn't continue coaching. He had no plans to quit or retire, and in fact couldn't afford to stop working.

We told the Moores that Davie's comments directly linking the firing to age and his stated belief that Joe could not last for the full five years of Davie's contract with Notre Dame, were certainly evidence of age discrimination under the 1967 Federal Age Discrimination in Employment Act. We had worked on many cases involving this statute, which outlawed employment decisions based on an employee's age and prohibited mandatory retirement: an employer cannot legally require that employees retire at age sixty-five or, indeed, at any age. The age discrimination law applied to universities, including coaching staffs, we told the Moores, and while a head coach was free to pick his own coaching staff, he could not make hiring or firing decisions based on a coach's age. Under the law, a head coach acts as a legal agent for the university; thus his actions in selecting a staff are fully covered by the Age Discrimination in Employment Act.

After the Moores left, we agreed, based on what we had just heard from two obviously genuine people, that here was a case of age discrimination. "We should at least try to get a settlement for them," I suggested. "I think the chances are excellent that we'll be able to quietly settle this case with Notre Dame. The last thing they want is a lawsuit from their offensive line coach." I knew that I was disregarding the firm's policy of not representing individuals in employment cases, but I thought that this case would not end in litigation because we would reach a quick, favorable resolution. I said I was going to contact Gerald Skoning, a friend who was a partner at Seyfarth, Shaw, Fairweather & Geraldson, a Chicago law firm that represented Notre Dame—and where I had been a partner thirteen years before—and suggest a quick meeting with the appropriate university officials to try to resolve the case. Since only a few days had elapsed since Moore's firing, we might even be able to get his job back.

Tim Klenk and I were confident that Notre Dame would be eager to settle the case quickly. During the past several years, our large corporate clients had become extremely concerned when employment discrimination cases by their former employees threatened to make a big splash in the media. Corporations were particularly leery of the damaging publicity that can be generated by class action discrimination suits— as in the cases of Texaco and Mitsubishi, where accusations of corporate race discrimination and sexual harassment resulted in embarrassing front-page headlines and ultimately led to public apologies by the companies as well as to large monetary settlements. After that, we kept getting calls from corporate clients who were worried that threatened employment discrimination claims would explode into highly publicized litigation.

I phoned Gerald Skoning, who confirmed that Seyfarth still represented Notre Dame in some employment matters. After briefly describing Moore's claim, I said that we would like to settle the matter and that I thought Notre Dame would like to do that as well, and that this informal back-door approach would keep the matter confidential. I hoped I was sending the message that, as a fellow management lawyer, I was sympathetic to Notre Dame and would work with them to reach a fair and private resolution to the case. I said that I was willing to drive to South Bend to meet with the appropriate officials, and stressed that speed was important because Moore wanted to return to his job. Skoning said he would call me back as soon as possible.

The next day, he left me a voice mail message telling me to call Notre Dame's General Counsel, Carol Kaesebier, in South Bend, to discuss the matter on the phone. This surprised me. Typically, settlement discussions for important cases are held face-to-face. A successful settlement is more likely when the parties meet personally, take each other's measure and have time to explore all facets of the case for potential settlement. A telephone call between total strangers is not as likely to lead to a resolution.

Tim Klenk and I decided to place the call together. Three years earlier Tim, then fifty-three years old, had merged his ten-lawyer labor and employment department with ours when his law firm had dissolved. He was soft-spoken and intellectual, revered by his clients for his integrity, his scholarly bent and his judgment. He suggested that we include one of our associates, thirty-year-old Mary Margaret (Mimi) Moore (no relation to Joe), in the phone call. While I hadn't yet worked with Mimi, I knew that Tim had a high opinion of her. She had graduated from St. Mary's, a private Catholic college across the street from Notre Dame, and her husband, a Notre Dame graduate, had been a student manager of the football team. So Tim thought that her firsthand knowledge of Notre Dame football could be helpful in settlement discussions.

Seven days after Moore's firing, Tim, Mimi and I gathered in my office to telephone Carol Kaesebier, the Notre Dame General Counsel. We had looked her up in the *Directory of Corporate Counsel*: she had been admitted to the bar in 1983, which probably meant she was around forty years old, had worked as counsel at Notre Dame for eight years and before that had been an associate lawyer with Barnes & Thornburg, a blue chip Indiana law firm. On the speaker phone, Tim told Kaesebier that we had met with Joe Moore two days before, and were anxious to resolve the matter as soon as possible because the coach loved Notre Dame, wanted to stay on in his job and hoped the university might reverse its decision before the story of his discharge became public. Tim outlined the facts of the case, including Davie's references to Moore's age. "In our opinion," he said, "this is a clear case of age discrimination."

"Joe misunderstood what happened," Kaesebier replied. "He has not been discharged; rather, he has a five-year employment contract with the university that will expire in two months and will not be renewed. This is simply a decision not to extend his contract—not age discrimination."

Mimi raised her eyebrows. Under the age discrimination law, a decision not to renew an employment contract because of age was illegal age discrimination—the same as refusing to hire or deciding to fire a person. I tried to explain this to Kaesebier, but she ignored me. She said that we should understand that it is standard procedure for a new head coach to replace his coaching staff at will. Tim protested that the head coach cannot replace his assistants when age is the reason for the decision. In this case, Davie expressly told Coach Moore that he was terminating him because he wanted someone younger.

Kaesebier replied that there were "performance issues" involving Moore's dealings with his peers. Trying to break the stalemate, Tim said that all Coach Moore wanted was to continue coaching at Notre Dame. Kaesebier said she didn't know if that would be possible. Father Beauchamp, the Notre Dame executive responsible for its athletic department, had already decided that they would pay Moore for a year and a half, but she would talk to him about our request.

After we hung up, I said that possibly Kaesebier did not appreciate the seriousness of the case, if she really thought that Moore's soon-to-expire contract with Notre Dame meant that his termination was not covered by the age discrimination laws. I had to believe that Notre Dame could not want a public lawsuit over this, and that Kaesebier would come back with a reasonable settlement offer.

We knew that putting a dollar value on the case would be difficult. Moore earned $79,500 for his final season, in addition to a $8,500 bowl bonus for the previous year. Under the Age Discrimination in Employment Act, a terminated employee can recover his lost wages up to the time of trial minus any earnings received from another job. He can also receive reinstatement to his job, if the job is still open. If reinstatement is not possible, the employee can sometimes recover front pay—an estimate of how much he would have earned in the future if he had remained employed. The law also provides for doubling of the back pay if the legal violation is "willful"; that is, in reckless disregard of the law. The big problem in this case was estimating Moore's wage loss. Since he had been fired only seven days before, all we could do was guess at how long he would be out of work and what compensation he was likely to receive in a new coaching position. However, since it was up to Notre Dame to respond to our offer to reinstate him, there was no need for us to estimate damages at this point.

Carol Kaesebier phoned Tim the next day to report that she had spoken with both Father Beauchamp and Bob Davie, who told her that Moore's contract had not been renewed because of "performance problems": his coaching methods were completely inconsistent with Davie's standards and the university's standards as well. Joe had engaged in "intimidation and physical abuse," showing a total lack of respect for the players. For example, she said, because he had made offensive remarks to a player who was praying during halftime, the player was transferring to another school. "There is no age discrimination here," she said flatly. Joe had jumped to that conclusion because a player had misunderstood something Davie had said at a meeting and had told his father that "Coach Moore is going to retire." As far as a resolution of this matter was concerned, Moore's return was not even a possibility, although Notre Dame "would listen to a financial offer."

"That's disappointing," Tim told her, "because Joe's real interest is to coach at Notre Dame."

There was a long pause. Mimi Moore went into Tim's office, and he pushed the speaker button so she could hear.

In a low, deliberate voice, Kaesebier said, "You should understand that if Joe files a lawsuit, a lot of bad things will come to light, including physical abuse and intimidation of players. He should carefully consider the negative publicity that will come out about him." She paused again to let her words sink in. "If he ever wants to coach again, he should think about things that he would not want to become public."

Taken aback by Kaesebier's implicit threat, Mimi and Tim exchanged glances.

"They didn't fire me because of mistreatment of players," Joe protested, after we told him what Kaesebier had said. "There was an incident two years ago where I slapped some kids in the locker room during halftime of an exhibition game. Holtz wrote a note telling me not to let it happen again, and it never did. I talked to Davie almost every day and he never, ever mentioned it. They didn't fire me for that reason!"

"Maybe it bothered Davie, but he never said anything to you," I suggested.

"It didn't bother Davie," he replied heatedly. "Davie just hired Jim Colletto, the head coach at Purdue, to replace me.

A player at Purdue sued Colletto for physical abuse. How can they say they fired me for slapping players two years ago and then hire a guy as my replacement who's been sued for physical abuse?"

"Kaesebier says your approach to coaching is inconsistent with their standards."

"Standards, what standards?" He was becoming even more upset. "Davie has no standards! He's been in all kinds of trouble during his coaching career. When he was coaching at Arizona, he got into some kind of legal trouble, I don't know the details. Then I heard that when he was at Tulane, he sent one of his assistants to spy on another team and there was trouble over that too." Attempting to control his emotions, he rasped, "After nine years, they tell me I'm too old to coach. Then, they tell the players that I'm retiring. Now they say I'm fired because I've abused players and didn't measure up to their standards. There is nothing more they can do to me."

Honesty—more than any other virtue—mattered to Joe. He would never tell a lie to his players. They trusted him and he trusted them. And throughout his career, he spoke his mind to his superiors, even when it was detrimental to his own advancement. In Joe's scheme of things, truth was far more important than money. In fact, money meant nothing to him. He never knew his salary, never signed a check, and never asked for a raise. Fran gave him spending money and managed their finances. In 1991, when Notre Dame asked Joe to make a five-year commitment, it was Fran who instructed him to get it in writing. Getting a contract never occurred to him, because he believed that Notre Dame's integrity matched his own. But when we told him of our conversation with Kaesebier, he changed his mind about that.

Tim, Mimi and I sat in our angular conference room. "Kaesebier didn't explicitly deny that Davie made age comments to Joe," Tim said. "What she seems to be saying is that abuse and intimidation of players were the main reasons or the real reasons for the firing." He reminded us of a U.S. Supreme Court case, *Price-Waterhouse v. Hopkins,* that dealt with a "mixed motive" defense where the employer is motivated by two reasons—one illegal and one legal—for firing an employee. If the legal reason is the main one for the firing, and the employee would have been fired even without the other, illegal, reason, the employer wins.

Tim suggested that Notre Dame was raising that mixed motive defense—relying on mistreatment of players as the overriding reason for the firing. Unless we could cast serious doubt on the reasons offered by Kaesebier, we would have no credibility in the settlement discussions. Under the age discrimination law, when an employer offers a legitimate reason for the firing, the legal burden is on the employee to show it is a "pretext"—an excuse designed to cover up the real, illegal reason. A demonstration that the employer has somehow behaved inconsistently or does not genuinely believe in the reason that it has given, is evidence of pretext. Without evidence of pretext, the employee cannot win the case.

Remembering Joe's comment that Notre Dame had just hired a Purdue coach who had been sued for player abuse, I asked, "How could Notre Dame have honestly fired Joe for mistreating players if they replaced him with a man who did the same thing or worse? Isn't that inconsistent with the discharge reason that Kaesebier gave us? And they said that Joe hadn't met their standards—but if Davie really did bad things himself in the past, the 'standards' defense seems bogus as well. So if we are going to have any credibility with a monetary settlement demand, we'd better confirm what Joe told us. And we better do it fast, before they decide that we haven't gotten back to her because they've blown us away."

That afternoon, sitting in front of her computer in her office, Mimi expertly worked her way through Westlaw, an on-line repository for millions of newspaper and magazine articles. I stopped in from time to time to see how she was doing. I no longer felt ambivalent about the case: Kaesebier's aggressive response had excited my natural combativeness; I had an instinctive feeling that Joe was an honest man and I was eager to learn if Mimi could find anything to corroborate what he had told us. After about three hours, she located newspaper articles on Jim Colletto and Bob Davie. Anxiously, I stood by her desk, reading over her shoulder.

Wire service stories dated August 4, 1993, reported that Purdue University had been sued by Ryan Harmon, a former Indiana high school football star and by Harmon's parents, who alleged that Head Coach Colletto had mentally and physically abused Harmon, an offensive lineman, who was "physically hit, punched, kicked and shoved with regularity as a method of coaching," had been called a variety of vulgar names by Colletto and had become suicidal because of this treatment.

Some players rose to Colletto's defense: one said that there was "always going to be some yelling and pushing on a football field, but I don't think [Harmon] was singled out. I don't think Coach [Colletto] singled him out more than anybody else." Another said that Harmon was "babied compared to other players" and that "Coach Colletto gets his point across. But I have no ill effects, it made me a better person." Nevertheless, in subsequent press reports, Colletto acknowledged that at least some of Harmon's charges were true: "I think a lot of them are out in left field. I will say that there were some things said to the youngster that I wasn't totally pleased with, but none that haven't been apologized for."

The *Indianapolis News* reported: "The University admitted Colletto and Harmon might have had some physical contact, [but] it said it was within the rules of football and the expectations between a player and a coach as part of football practice." A sports reporter for the *Star* opined that Colletto, who was known as an "intimidation freak," had unwittingly crossed the line in his treatment of Harmon. Purdue players, past and present, commented on Colletto's reputation as a fiery, intense, in-your-face coach.

The Ryan Harmon case touched off a national media debate on the line between appropriate and inappropriate behavior by a college football coach. Features appeared on the ESPN cable network, in *USA Today* and in the sports sections of newspapers throughout the Midwest. Michigan's head football coach said that while he did not believe in abuse, "If you're going to have your son go into the service, you want some tough son of a gun as a drill sergeant coaching him before he goes up on those front lines and needs to know how to survive. Football is not how to survive, but it's a tough physical game where you have to have some toughness and physicalness taught you." Indiana's head coach said, "It's a tough game, and there's got to be a toughness there. It's a good old hard-nosed, kick-rump game. But again, there's a fine line there. You can't go overboard as a coach."

On February 15, 1994, the press reported that Harmon had dropped his case. "The allegations stand and are still true," Harmon said, but "the justice system isn't the way I can get my justice in this." He said he was satisfied that his case had brought about positive changes at Purdue, at least. "Some good has come from it. Since I filed this and went on ESPN, Jim Colletto has straightened up. I didn't want the money out of this. I wanted this stopped at the college level. It's still going on, but hopefully at Purdue it straightened up somewhat."

Excited, I said, "This is just what we hoped to find. Notre Dame claims they fired Moore over some minor incident, and then they turn around and replace him with an intimidation freak who was involved in a nationally reported player abuse suit. If that isn't legal pretext defense, I don't know what is."

"Yes, but Rick," Mimi said, "what if Notre Dame didn't know about Colletto's reputation or the Harmon case when they hired him? I mean, it's hard to believe they didn't know since college football coaching is a pretty small world and this got a lot of publicity. But it doesn't help us if they didn't know about it."

I couldn't accept this. "They must do a reference check before they hire people. Clearly, Notre Dame had to know about Colletto's hard-nose style and they hired him anyway. And if they really cared about what Moore did, they would have fired him right after that slapping incident two years ago. It's all a bunch of bullshit. Davie just thought Moore was too old to coach, and now they're scrambling to cover it up."

"It looks like Davie has some past experience in covering up." Mimi handed me a newspaper story, dated October 23, 1984, about a lawsuit brought by Gerald Materne, a former volunteer football coach, against Tulane University, its head coach Wally English and defensive coordinator Bob Davie, seeking $988,000 for damage to his reputation caused by being fired for spying on a Mississippi State University practice session. Materne claimed that he was sent to Starkeville, Mississippi, on a spying mission by Davie and English immediately before Tulane's season opener at Mississippi State.

Mimi explained that spying on a team's closed practice was a cardinal sin in college football. "I don't know if it's an NCAA violation, but it's considered highly improper."

Materne was caught in the spying mission and told by the campus police that he would be jailed for trespassing if he ever came back. "So apparently Materne claimed that Davie and the head coach participated in a crime—even if it was only a minor one—by instructing him to trespass at Mississippi State," I said.

"Keep reading, Rick, it gets sleazier."

The lawsuit alleged that Davie arranged a meeting with Materne and English "to coordinate their public position" and "fabricated a story for release to the press" that Materne had acted on his own initiative without the knowledge of English and Davie. At first, reporters were told that Materne had quit his job, which wasn't true, but later, when the embarrassment grew more intense, the university fired Materne.

The basis of the suit was that English and Davie had caused Materne's firing and the adverse publicity had jeopardized his ability to earn a livelihood in the coaching profession.

"Amazing! This is a cover-up—a football Watergate!" I said.

"Well, we don't know whether this is true, but it certainly sounds as if Davie has an interesting past," Mimi said. "And there's definitely a pattern here. Look at this." She handed me a printout of a *South Bend Tribune* story dated December 6, 1996, only six days earlier. The story, headed "Davie Admits Early Career Error," reported that Davie had been indicted on seven different criminal fraud and conspiracy charges in 1980 when he was a football coach at the University of Arizona. He was one of seven Arizona coaches, including the head coach, indicted on eighty-eight felony counts. The coaches were charged with bilking the university out of over $13,000 by filing phony airline receipts for recruiting trips. Davie was accused of turning in airline coupons for payment for plane trips for which he had already been reimbursed. The indictments were precipitated by a series of Pulitzer Prize–winning newspaper investigations.

Following the indictment, Davie took a job at the University of Pittsburgh and later sent Arizona a check for $1,285 to make restitution. He told the press, "In hindsight, I knew early on that it was a mistake. I dealt with it and learned from it. It never came up again."

Ultimately Arizona's head coach was acquitted and the charges against the other coaches, including Davie, were dropped. The *Tribune* article concluded that the episode was "college football's version of the White House" where "like the President, Davie now confronts the reality that fine print in his past may become bold headlines in his present." Davie was quoted as saying that Notre Dame's athletic director, Mike Wadsworth, and his superior, Father Beauchamp, "were totally aware of this and totally comfortable with this the entire time."

We were stunned. How could Notre Dame, a paragon of everything virtuous in college football, appoint a head coach with a criminal indictment in his past? And how could they contend seriously that Moore did not meet their standards when they had appointed Bob Davie with his history? The explanation offered by Kaesebier for Moore's firing certainly appeared to be pretextual under the age discrimination law.

"How," Tim asked, "could their General Counsel come up with a settlement strategy like this? First she says that it's not age discrimination because they didn't renew his contract—she says this even though she must know that refusal to renew someone's contract because of age violates the law. Then she completely shifts gears and raises this defense about abuse and standards which is incredible in light of the Colletto hiring and Davie's past. But what really amazes me is that she's putting their dirty laundry smack in the middle of any potential legal proceedings."

Kaesebier's defense altered our assessment of the case. What had originally appeared to be a simple age discrimination case now involved damaging information about Bob Davie, Jim Colletto and Notre Dame itself. "When we call Kaesebier, I'll bet she will be shocked by this information," I said.

We continued to puzzle over how to value the case. It was impossible, only a week after Moore's firing, to determine how long he would be unemployed and what kind of earnings, if any, he would receive elsewhere. Tim suggested that, as an opening offer to Notre Dame, we should base our settlement number on the maximum potential recovery and let Notre Dame counteroffer. On the assumption that Moore could work another twelve years, and that a jury would find a "willful" termination which would double his back pay recovery, Tim suggested that we make an opening offer of 1.3 million, and that we probably would not settle for less than $200,000—about two years of lost wages. Ultimately, however, it was Joe Moore who would decide on the bottom-line settlement amount.

The next day we phoned Kaesebier. Tim dwelt on how much pain Notre Dame had inflicted on Coach Moore by the way the firing was handled and by the allegations of player abuse against him. Kaesebier's response was conciliatory. Davie, she said, certainly had not intended to hurt Joe's feelings; he was trying help Joe to save his dignity and to avoid a confrontation. It was true, she went on, that Davie had said that he needed someone who would be there through the entire five years of his contract and she understood that there could be a question about how Joe would react to that. But there was no question that Notre Dame had handled the discharge correctly and legally.

When I told her what we had discovered about Colletto and Davie, she immediately became combative: "Davie has a right to hire any offensive coach he wants. If Colletto and Davie did something improper in their past, it didn't happen at Notre Dame. What we are talking about is performance at Notre Dame, not at some other place. Whatever you claim they did, it did not happen here. We will not hire Coach Moore back, if that's what this conversation is all about. If that's what you want, this is a waste of time. You can dig up all the dirt you want. Davie can retain or dismiss anybody he wants for his staff."

Tim attempted to defuse the tension. "We do understand that the university won't bring Joe back," he calmly stated. "We are prepared to make a monetary offer." He paused, but she didn't say anything. "Since Coach Moore can't return to his position at Notre Dame, we are requesting compensation for the remainder of his working life, which we estimate at 1.3 million dollars. Carol, please consider this and let us know." There was silence on the other end, and then she that said she would get back to us.

After three days with no response, we decided to fax a letter informing Kaesebier that our offer would be withdrawn at noon on the following day. Several hours later, she phoned to tell Tim curtly that she had responded days ago by leaving a message with his secretary. Tim said that he never received the message. "In any event," Kaesebier said, "Notre Dame has no counteroffer. Coach Moore will have to do what he finds appropriate. We will pay him until June of this year. By the way, as to your claim about Bob Davie at Tulane, we checked it out with them. It's completely untrue."

Settlement talks had clearly broken down. Now I had to decide whether we should pursue this case. It was one thing for a management law firm to help Joe to a quiet settlement; it was quite another to undertake an actual lawsuit, particularly where there was likely to be a lot of publicity. I was also worried because several important Ross & Hardies clients had high-level executives who were Notre Dame graduates. Given the intense loyalty of Notre Dame alumni, they might disapprove of the firm's involvement in a case against their alma mater. The case might also damage the firm's reputation with its other corporate clients. And there was the question of money. We could lose the case after we spent hundreds of thousands of dollars to fund it. From a business standpoint, it simply made no sense to proceed.

On the other hand, I believed that Notre Dame was bluffing, and had no intention of litigating the case. Kaesebier's strategy seemed designed to frighten us off by threatening to destroy Moore's reputation if he sued. Once Notre Dame understood that we intended to take the case forward, I was certain that they would settle. So I felt that we should go on with it. I recognized that this was to some extent a decision based on a visceral response, but I believed that we could run the case with the steadfast focus on the economic bottom line that characterized our corporate practice. I was a business lawyer and the business at hand was to obtain a good recovery for my client and my firm. I had always been a practical person and although I may not have made a practical decision in taking this case, I was determined that it was going to be handled in a practical way.

My life, it seemed, had been comprised of a series of careful steps. I had entered the University of Cincinnati Law School after switching from pre-med (my father was a doctor and I wanted to please him by following in his footsteps, but organic chemistry defeated me) to liberal arts at Miami University. I found most of the law school courses dry and uninspiring. However, during a summer internship with a

Cincinnati law firm, I was assigned a labor law project that changed my attitude. It was an arbitration case concerning the question of whether a union job should include the employment of a particular welding device. This might not seem to be the type of legal matter that would excite a young law student, but as I sat at the counsel table, observing management and labor fighting over control of the welding task, I began to understand the intensity of the human struggle that could arise from an individual's need to make a living and a corporation's need to make a profit.

So, during my final year in law school, I took the only available labor law course, and after graduation, went to work for the National Labor Relations Board, traditional training ground for an aspiring labor lawyer. From there I went on to a job with the Equal Employment Opportunity Commission (EEOC) which had just received Congressional authority to prosecute employment discrimination cases. I hoped that this experience would give me an edge over young aspiring labor lawyers, and it did. After a year and a half with the EEOC, I became an associate and then a partner at Seyfarth, Shaw.

I stayed with that firm for nine years. I had carefully and conservatively planned the evolution of my career to work my way into a completely secure partnership with a top firm, so when Ross & Hardies offered me the opportunity to set up a labor and employment department for them, I agonized over the decision. I did not want to risk everything I had worked for, but I also did not want to be limited to a predictable professional life with the same clients, legal work and lock-step salary increases until I retired. I was not a risk taker, but I decided to take the risk. I accepted the partnership at Ross & Hardies, bringing along a junior associate from my former firm. Every one of my clients followed me.

Over the next thirteen years, my department grew to twenty-five lawyers; I was elected to the firm's executive committee, and served for several years as its managing partner. I had exceeded all my professional goals. Now, for reasons I couldn't quite fathom, I decided to take a risk on the Moore case. Of course, I told myself, it was a limited risk: I was banking on a good settlement offer from Notre Dame once it was understood that the alternative was a high-profile destructive legal action.

But before filing the action, we had to investigate further. Rule 11 of the Federal Rules of Civil Procedure requires that all lawsuits brought in federal court must have evidentiary support. Attorneys who file lawsuits without verifying the factual claims, are subject to monetary sanctions against them and/or their client and even to dismissal of the lawsuit.

Kaesebier had made several critical challenges to our claims. She denied that there had been age discrimination and that Davie had been involved in the spying incident at Tulane. Although we felt certain that we had a case on the basis of Davie's specific age-related comments to Moore at his home, the problem was that it was Davie's word against the Moores'. The head coach of Notre Dame would carry a great deal of moral authority before a jury, which could readily believe Davie over an angry ex-employee and his wife. To satisfy Rule 11 and have the factual support to force a settlement, we needed more evidence of age discrimination, and that evidence had to be gathered before the lawsuit was filed. We also needed to verify the claims about Davie's past.

By late December, the Moores were making plans to sell their South Bend apartment and move back to Pittsburgh near family. During the weeks since his firing, Joe received call after call of support from friends and coaches at other schools. But he heard nothing from his former colleagues at Notre Dame. An iron curtain seemed to have descended between himself and the university. A few days before Christmas, a friend brought Joe the January edition of the *Blue and Gold Illustrated*, a newspaper covering Notre Dame football. There were two long articles about Joe's departure by Tim Prister, the newspaper's editor and principal writer. Although Joe knew that the *Blue and Gold* would favor Notre Dame in any controversy, since it was dependent on the university's good will for access to the coaches and players, he was not prepared for what he read.

Prister wrote that "an apparent misunderstanding" over what was said to the offensive linemen about Joe's termination provoked "a fiery exit by the 64-year-old coaching legend. . . . A day after his firing, Moore erupted in the football office as he returned to gather his belongings [and went on] a rampage spewing dirty laundry on the basis of a freshman's misinterpretation of Davie's talk with the offensive linesmen." Prister's point was that "Davie had little choice with Moore" since Moore's relationship with Lou Holtz, the former head coach, had deteriorated to the point that Holtz had to take over the coaching of offensive tackles earlier that fall as "damage control": players, coaches, trainers and student managers would gather around Holtz at the conclusion of each practice, and "Moore would wander off on his own agenda. . . . At age 64, Moore no longer was physically capable of putting in the hours of his coaching cohorts, and had long ago abandoned an 'all-for-one, one-for-all' approach."

Davie's remarks about Joe's age were treated as innocuous observations. Davie was quoted as saying that one of the main reasons for the firing was that Joe didn't plan to continue coaching through Davie's five-year contract: "But in my opinion, Joe was not going to coach more than one or two more years. He even said that. Continuity on this staff is very important, and I made a decision based upon the long-range interest of the program. That's exactly what I told the offensive linemen."

Joe knew that the *Blue and Gold* was read by college football professionals. This statement that he was no longer physically capable of coaching and had lost Holtz's confidence would have a devastating effect on his chances of landing a good coaching position anywhere.

"They're trying to destroy me," Joe told Fran.

When we read these articles, we concluded that Notre Dame had launched a preemptive strike. Davie's reference to Moore's supposed intent not to coach more than one or two more years, was obviously the spin the university intended to put on age-related comments. Part of the defense was going to be that Davie did not fire Moore because of his age, but chose not to renew his contract because Moore said he was going to leave coaching in a year or two, and Davie needed a five-year commitment that would parallel his own contract. We decided to conduct legal research on whether an employer's desire for "continuity"—employees who will stay for a number of years—is a valid defense to an age discrimination case. We also considered whether the reporter's statements that Moore was no longer physically capable at age sixty-four and had abandoned the all-for-one approach, were defamatory under Indiana law. This might be more than an age discrimination case.

I phoned Joe to ask him whether he had really told people he intended to quit coaching in a year or two.

"Not in the way Davie describes it in the paper," Joe said. "The last few years working under Holtz was rough for all of the assistant coaches. The administration, particularly Wadsworth, the new athletic director, was driving Holtz crazy, second guessing everything he did. They were trying to make him leave. Holtz took it out on everyone—coaches and players. A lot of the coaches started to talk about getting other jobs and some of them did. Davie complained to me all the time about Holtz—he said he hated him, he despised him. In fact, it was Davie who was planning to leave to get a head coaching job somewhere. But not me—I had no intention of leaving. I may have said what the other coaches were saying—if things didn't improve, I'd leave. But I wasn't going to retire. I couldn't retire if I wanted to. We don't have money. Anyway, I love coaching. As long as I can get a job, I'll coach."

"What about Holtz taking over coaching your offensive tackles?"

"Holtz never took over my job. All he did was meet with the tackles for about twenty minutes a day, a couple of days a week during the early part of last season. That was his only involvement and he even stopped doing that later in the season. I always had a good relationship with Holtz and I know he respected me." He paused. "So tell me Rick, how does my case look?"

I told him his case looked good, but we had some work to do.

The Ross & Hardies library ordered photocopies of 1983 and 1984 articles from New Orleans and Mississippi newspapers that were not available on Westlaw. The spying incident had been a big scandal. The *New Orleans Times-Picayune* gave the story extensive coverage, calling it "Wallygate" after Tulane's head coach Wally English, who contended that he did not authorize graduate assistant Gerry Materne's spying trip to Mississippi, that Materne had acted on his own and had subsequently resigned. The *Times-Picayune* was skeptical: "If you for a moment believe the kid peeped on his own, well, let's the two of us get together. I've got these three gorgeous acres I'd like to sell." The reporter commented that while the NCAA does not have rules against clandestine operations, such conduct in college football is considered "unethical as Hades, to be sure."

We clearly needed to talk to Materne. If Davie was implicated in this story of lies, deceit and cover-up, it would be evidence that Notre Dame's claim that Joe did not meet its standards was nothing more than pretext. It could also carry an important subtext to a jury—that Davie lacked credibility. The problem was finding Materne twelve years after the incident.

We got the name and phone number of Materne's attorney, John Seago, from the 1984 court papers. When I phoned him, Seago said that he certainly remembered the case. It had generated a great deal of newspaper coverage, and soon after the lawsuit was filed, it was settled under confidential terms. Seago believed that Materne had a very good case, but had decided to take a fair offer by Tulane to put the matter behind him. He had moved from New Orleans years ago and Seago didn't know where he lived.

Seago's belief in Materne's claims was not enough to eliminate the risk of violating Rule 11. We had to interview Materne himself. Before the advent of on-line research, we would be at a dead end; Materne could be living anywhere. Mimi surfed the Internet for search engines that could find him. After some trial and error, she came across a long list of Gerald Maternes, including addresses and ages. Gerald Materne, age 40, of Lacomb, Louisiana, looked promising. When a woman answered the phone, Mimi asked if this was the residence of the Gerald Materne who had coached at Tulane. The woman hesitated and then said that he was her husband, and would be home later that evening.

Mimi raced down the hallway to my office. "I found him! He lives in a small town in Louisiana and we can call him tonight!"

Mrs. Materne didn't mention the phone call to her husband, so he was taken aback to get a call from two lawyers in Chicago asking, "Are you the Gerry Materne who coached at Tulane?" Materne was now a successful financial planner who specialized in investment advice to physicians. Long ago he had given up his dream of becoming a college football coach.

After graduating from Louisiana State University, he was hired by Louisiana State as a graduate assistant football coach—the traditional entry-level job in college coaching.

Unfortunately, the head coach at LSU, Bo Ryan, was killed
in a plane crash about three months after Materne was hired
and the new coach let Materne go. He tried a sales job for
two years, but he desperately wanted to get back into coaching, so he took a $12,000-a-year job coaching and teaching
at Holy Cross High School in New Orleans. This was not
enough money to support his wife and new baby; in order to
make ends meet, he operated a pest control business eve-
nings and on weekends.

In the summer of 1983, Tulane University hired a new
coach, Wally English. Materne saw English and his new
coaching staff on television. He was impressed because they
typified the new breed of preppy coaches, wearing ties and
blazers over starched white shirts with button-down collars.
Described by the local media as business coaches, they were
completely unlike the old-line coaches who wore sweatshirts
and chewed gum. In June, 1983, Materne drove over to
Tulane and introduced himself to English. "I've been coaching at Holy Cross High School. I'd like to get into college
coaching. I used to coach at LSU. Do you have a spot for
me? I'll come here and work for free."

Several days later, English telephoned Materne. "We have
a spot. You can coach on the defense because we don't have
a graduate assistant there. But I can't pay you at first."

Materne and his wife had about $5,000 in the bank. They
decided that if they lived as frugally as possible and saved
every penny, they could exist on those savings for about six
months, which would take them to the end of the football
season. If he didn't get a paying job by that time, he would
have to abandon his dream.

Seven months later when Materne's coaching hopes had been crushed, he fell into depression. But as he became more and more successful in his new career as a financial consultant, he decided that God had a plan, and the plan was that Gerald Materne was not meant to be a football coach. Things happened for a reason and the death of the head coach at LSU, followed by the spying scandal, was part of the plan. His wife told him many times that he was so hard-headed, it took God hitting him over the head with a two-by-four to get him out of coaching.

Materne now owned an expensive contemporary home on a golf course. He had two children and a life with plenty of discretionary time. Our phone call, asking him out of the blue to resurrect the events that had ended his dream of college coaching, was an unwelcome surprise. That we were lawyers for the Notre Dame offensive line coach, looking into a possible lawsuit against Bob Davie, was even more startling. Materne had hated Bob Davie for a long time because he felt that Davie had used him. But he believed that he had long ago put that behind him, and when he read that Davie received the head coaching job at Notre Dame, Materne told his family that he intended to write Davie a congratulatory note because things had worked out well for both of them.

Now we were asking him about that chapter in his life that he wanted to forget. As he considered simply hanging up on us, he thought about the similarities between what had happened to him and what was happening to Joe Moore: even though Moore had been Davie's long-time colleague, as soon as he became head coach, Davie fired him because he thought he was too old for the job. Davie screwed me and hung me out to dry thirteen years ago, Materne thought, and now he's done it to somebody else. He decided he had nothing to lose. He would tell us what happened.

II

———

1983–84: TULANE

In the summer of 1983, Gerald Materne landed a job as graduate assistant on the defensive coaching staff at Tulane. His boss was Bob Davie, the new defensive coordinator: Materne idolized him. Only a few years older than Materne, Davie was already a coach in a big time college football program. He was handsome, smooth and ambitious, and was sure that he would be a head coach by the time he was thirty-five. Materne was convinced that with his Ivy League appearance, self-confidence and intense drive to succeed, Davie would surely achieve his goal.

Tulane's first opponent of the season was Mississippi State; Davie worried that Mississippi would use different formations from those Tulane expected. Formations are the patterns that the offense uses during the game. This was Davie's first job as defensive coordinator and he wanted to do "a good job first time out of the box." The defensive coach should know, well in advance, how the other teams' offensive players will line up, so that he can train his defensive players to counter them. The Tulane defensive coaches had closely studied films of MSU's formations from the previous

year, but there was no guarantee that Mississippi would use
the same formations this time.

When Davie first raised the idea of spying on Mississippi, it seemed to be a joke. During a meeting with the five
members of the defensive coaching staff, he said, "We have
absolutely no idea what they're going to do. It would sure be
nice to know. We need to go spy on them." Everyone laughed.
But a few days later, he raised the subject again. "You know,
we ought to send Materne here to spy on Mississippi State.
He's a real aggressive guy."

Materne grinned, thinking Davie was referring to the fact
that he had walked into Tulane off the street, introduced
himself and convinced them to hire him. "Yeah, yeah. I'll
just go spy. I'll be like the CIA." But Davie did not let the
matter go. A few days later, he told the defensive coaching
staff, "I'm really afraid that we're not preparing this team
properly." He turned to Materne. "You know, we really ought
to send you to spy." Materne realized that Davie was serious. Eager to please his new colleagues, he said he would do
it.

Materne knew that spying on another team is unethical.
While he didn't know what, if any, specific NCAA rules applied, he understood that spying violated the basic principles
of college football, and anyone caught doing it would probably be banned from college coaching.

In early August, the Tulane football team moved to training camp in rural Gulfport, Mississippi, where the players
and coaches would live for several weeks to concentrate,
uninterrupted, on practice and preparation. At the camp,
Davie went on openly discussing the spying mission. Materne,

despite misgivings, told Davie, "Well, that's what I'm here for. I'm here to help you. If you really feel like that's what we need to do, I'll do it."

Materne and Davie discussed the logistics of the mission. Materne owned an old Datsun B-210; he was afraid that it wouldn't make the six-hour drive to Starkeville, Mississippi, and back, so Davie lent him his own car.

One day after practice, Davie invited Materne into the coaching room and began to write down the formations and other information he wanted Materne to get for him. He was particularly interested in Mississippi's tight end, Danny Knight, an all-American offensive player, whom Davie viewed as a significant threat to Tulane. He wanted Materne to find out where Knight, No. 22, would be placed in the offensive formation. He stressed to Materne that knowledge of Mississippi's cadence—what the quarterback says when he starts the play—was critical. To hear the cadence, Materne would have to position himself very close to the players during the practice. When Davie finished writing, he gave Materne the paper containing a detailed set of instructions about getting information on line splits, shifts and motion. The next day during the second practice, as the players were warming up, Materne saw Head Coach Wally English walk over to Davie and give him money. After the practice, Davie handed Materne five $20 bills and his car keys, and said he would see him in a few days.

Materne had already discussed the spying plan with his wife. After leaving training camp, he phoned her in New Orleans to tell her he was about to go on the three-day mission. She told him that there was no way she would stay home alone—she had to come along with the baby. Materne left Gulfport in the late afternoon, drove forty minutes to New Orleans to pick up his wife and baby and then set off on the long drive in the dark over winding country roads. It was the most miserable trip of Materne's life. Leaving New Orleans around 6:30 P.M., he told his wife to make sure he stayed awake and did not doze off as he negotiated the pitch-black roads. They stopped several times for coffee and food, arriving in Starkeville at five in the morning, and checked into a small motel. Materne left a wake-up call for 7:30 A.M.

He left the motel that morning confident that he would not get caught. He had always had an ability to go into a place and act as if he fit right in. He parked the car about a mile from the Mississippi State campus, and got out, leaving his wallet in the glove compartment. He was wearing a baggy shirt to hide the binoculars tucked into his short sweatpants. It took a while to locate the athletic building complex, walk into the building and find the football varsity locker room. On the blackboard was a series of plays which he hurriedly copied onto the back of Davie's instruction sheet. To his delight, most of the formations on the blackboard were identical to the formations on Davie's sheet.

Leaving the building, he hurried through the campus, across a road and into the woods leading to the practice field. From the woods, he had a clear view of the players on the field. So he sat and watched, checking the formations that Davie wanted, and looking for No. 22, Danny Knight. Materne was too far away to hear the quarterback's cadence, but that didn't worry him because he had two or three more days to get closer to the field. As he was making notes, he heard noises in the bushes. It made no sense for people to be crashing through the bushes that early in the morning. He panicked, and turned to run back through the woods. He sprinted at full speed for about a quarter of a mile, running uphill when he reached the road. At the crest of the hill, he saw a man in MSU athletic garb coming toward him and another closing in behind him. Exhausted, he sank down on the curb and tried to catch his breath. The two men, MSU trainers, towered over him. Catching sight of the binoculars, they began firing questions at him: "What are you doing here? What are those binoculars for? What's going on?"

Still gasping for breath, Materne sat staring at the pavement. Within minutes, a campus police car pulled up. Materne told the two policemen that he was a high school coach who wanted to watch a college team so he could pick up pointers. When they asked for identification, Materne said that he didn't have his wallet with him.

"Well, I tell you what, you've got two choices," one of them said. "Identify yourself or go to jail."

Feeling as if he was in the midst of a nightmare, he said, "Go to jail? For what?"

"You're criminally trespassing."

At that point, he gave up and told them everything. They shoved him into the back of their vehicle and drove him to where he had parked Davie's car. He took his wallet out of the glove compartment and showed them his driver's license. The policemen wrote down that information along with Davie's plate number. They said, "Get the hell out of here and don't ever come back."

During the long drive back to New Orleans with his wife and baby, Materne tuned on WWL—a New Orleans radio station with a wide broadcasting range—and heard sports-

caster Hap Glaudi announce, "Gerald Materne, a Tulane
football coach, has been caught spying at Mississippi State."
Materne was stunned; it had just happened two hours ago
and already it was on the news.

As soon as they got home, around 5:00 that afternoon,
he fell into bed. Davie phoned several times, and each time
Mrs. Materne told him that her husband hadn't gotten back
yet. When he woke later in the evening, he was too depressed
to return Davie's call because he felt he had let the coach
down. But he answered when Davie phoned again around
eleven that night, and asked, "Man, what happened?"
Materne said that he had no idea how he had gotten caught.

"Well, let me ask you a question. Did you see anything?"

Materne told him that MSU's formations were pretty
much what Tulane had expected. "Now, listen," Davie said,
"don't talk to any reporters. What you have to do is get here
first thing in the morning because we've got to meet with
Wally and we've got to straighten our story out. We all have
to be telling the same story here because Wally's been getting
a lot of phone calls from the press and they want to know
what's going on. We've just been telling them that we don't
know anything."

The next morning, Davie, Wally English and Materne
met in one of Tulane's coaching rooms. English said, "You
know, Gerry, we've really got to get our story straight here
because Hindman Wall, the athletic director, doesn't like me;
he's looking for a reason to fire me and the entire coaching
staff. Why don't you just tell Wall that this was all your idea?
You're just a graduate assistant and that's not gonna be that
big a deal. You might have to leave for a little while, but

we'll get you back. It might be a big deal now, but in a few weeks nobody's even gonna remember it."

English and Davie told Materne to say he was an eager graduate assistant football coach who wanted to impress the coaching staff; that he had asked Davie if he could use his car to take care of his pest control business and that without their knowledge, he drove to Mississippi State to gather intelligence for the first game of the season. If he told this story, English and Davie promised that they would get him a paid coaching position on the staff when the commotion died down.

Accordingly, Materne met with Wall, and told him the fabricated story. Wall didn't buy it. "Why don't you tell me what really happened?" he asked. Materne insisted that the whole thing was his idea. Wall shook his head. "Son, I've been in this business for a long time, and I know that you didn't do this on your own. I don't believe you for one second. You're just making a terrible mistake covering for these guys because they've put you in a bad position."

Wall's words troubled Materne, but he felt he had to rely on English's explanation that Wall hated the coaching staff and wanted to get rid of them. This was the first time Materne had met Wall, but he knew and trusted Davie, who was his good friend, so he kept insisting that it was all his idea. "Well, I'll tell you something," Wall said, "you're not staying here to coach. You're out of here. We can't have coaches like you hanging around."

For the rest of the season, on weekends when only players and coaches were present, Materne worked secretly for

Tulane, breaking down film and doing grunt work. English told him that he'd help him financially if he needed help, but Materne had saved enough money to get through the football season. But the spying scandal did not die away. Tulane had become an object of ridicule. At the LSU game, the opposing team's mascot, Mike the Tiger, came onto the football field with giant binoculars and bushes around his shoulders.

Materne was interviewed by investigators from the NCAA and held tight to his story. At Davie's insistence, Materne agreed to an interview with the *New Orleans Times-Picayune*, telling the reporter that he had acted independently. Davie and English repeatedly reassured him they would take care of him when the scandal blew over. "Don't worry. Be patient," Davie said. "We'll take care of you financially and we'll make sure you get a coaching job. You will get a coaching job out of this."

In January, 1984, after the football season ended, Materne, at English's suggestion, attended a national college coaching convention at the Hyatt Regency Hotel in Dallas, where assistant coaches made contacts and tried to line up new jobs. English and Davie were both there and promised Materne that they would help him get a job. On the first day, English introduced Materne to several coaches, but no interviews followed. While English appeared to be making efforts for Materne, Davie did absolutely nothing; Materne couldn't even find him. On the third and last day of the convention, he finally spotted Davie in the hotel lobby, and went up to him. "Where have you been?" Materne demanded.

"You know, I've been around," Davie said.

Suddenly Materne realized that Davie had been avoiding him for days. "Well, you haven't introduced me to anybody! Remember the deal? I would take care of you and you would help me find a coaching job."

"Fuck you," replied Davie. "You're the asshole who got caught and I'm not helping you find anything."

Materne was stunned. Bob Davie, who he believed was his great friend, had used him. He had covered for Davie, had been steadfastly loyal to him, and when it came time for Davie to perform, he was welshing on his promise.

Materne told English what Davie had done. "You must have misunderstood," English reassured him. "I don't think he really meant that."

Materne insisted that Davie meant it. English, trying to calm him down, said, "Listen, Gerry, I want to give you a job. I've got an opening as an administrative assistant recruiting coordinator and you'd be great for it. I want you to have it."

Materne didn't hesitate. "Well, I want it. Okay, that's great, I'll take that job."

When Materne came back to New Orleans, English provided the details—a $25,000-a-year position as the head coach's administrative assistant and recruiting coordinator. But several days later, English phoned him again. "I've got bad news. I talked to Hindman Wall about your coming back and he said you can't come back because of the spy incident."

Materne met with Wall to ask why he had vetoed him.

"Son, you can't come back here. You embarrassed the university," Wall said. Materne, distraught, asked him if there was anything he could do to be reinstated at Tulane. "If you want to come back," Wall said, "tell me the truth."

Desperate, Materne told him the whole sordid story. Wall shook his head. "Well, you know, son, it's a shame that you lost your coaching career because of something as stupid as this. I'll do everything I can to get you back here, but what you have to do for me is first talk to my boss, Chuck Knapp."

Materne met with Knapp, told him everything, and gave him a copy of Davie's instruction sheet. Knapp said that there would be an internal audit and he'd get back to him in a few weeks. Weeks passed and neither Wall nor Knapp called. Materne phoned Wall's office, but he never responded. Shut out and betrayed by everyone, Materne wanted revenge. A friend referred him to a lawyer, John Seago, who filed a civil lawsuit against Davie, English and Tulane. Tulane quickly settled the case for $27,000. Materne received $20,000, which he used to replenish the savings he had used to support his family during the fiasco, and took a job as an insurance agent for Mutual of New York.

On his desk he kept a coffee mug that he had gotten at the Dallas convention, with "1984 College Coaching Convention/Puma Shoes," printed on it. Every time he was rejected by a potential customer—a common occurrence in the early days—he looked at the cup and repeated to himself, "I'm not going to let those guys beat me." Over the years, that mug helped him summon the fortitude, after each rejection, to persevere and call the next business prospect.

III

JANUARY–FEBRUARY 1997:
PREPARING THE LAWSUIT

We were of course very pleased with Materne's information but we considered it equally important to verify the abuse allegations about Jim Colletto at Purdue. If it was true that Notre Dame had hired Colletto knowing his reputation for mistreating players, that should certainly damage the defense argument that Moore was fired for similar conduct.

Our initial inquiries into the lawsuit brought by Ryan Harmon against Colletto were not promising. When I phoned Harmon's attorney, he told me that he had developed "a difference of opinion" with Harmon, and another lawyer had taken over the case. He told me only that several depositions were taken, and gave me the court reporter's name and phone number. The reporter told me that Indiana law precluded her from providing us with copies of the depositions. However, she remembered the case well and believed Ryan Harmon had dropped the lawsuit. Based on what had she heard at the depositions, she thought that Harmon was simply a "big baby."

Mimi and I next tried to find Harmon in his home town, Martinsville, Indiana. We located Harmon's father, a high school guidance counselor, who said his son no longer lived there. When we told him why we were calling, Mr. Harmon said, "I would like to kill Colletto!" He went on to tell us that Ryan, as a good Christian, had turned the terrible experience into a "positive" in his life, but he himself still had a difficult time with what had happened. Colletto had hit, kicked and tormented his son, almost ruining his life. Mr. Harmon said he had felt a moral obligation to encourage Ryan to sue Colletto, but eventually their lawyer told them that it could take up to five years and be very expensive to bring the case to conclusion. So Ryan decided to drop it and get on with his life. Mr. Harmon gave us no details of the abuse, but he did say that Colletto's actions were not limited to Ryan: on one occasion the coach went "nuts" in the locker room during a game and had to be restrained. Mr. Harmon wouldn't give us Ryan's telephone number, but he told us that his son was now an Indiana state trooper stationed near South Bend.

Ryan Harmon's phone number was listed with Information. He didn't seem surprised to hear from us, and he readily answered our questions. He said that he had been an All-American high school player and was Colletto's first recruit in 1991 after he was appointed head coach at Purdue. In his freshman year, Ryan was "red-shirted"—allowed to practice with the team but not permitted to play—and had limited involvement with Colletto. The following year, however, he was placed on the second team. At first Ryan thought Colletto was just a hard-line, "hands-on" coach. But he soon learned that Colletto's actions on the practice field were cruel. The coach had a practice of smashing his body into players as they stood on the field looking in the other direction. When they fell, he kicked them. Colletto often beat players with a helmet. Ryan, who considered himself a good Christian, had never heard the kind of language that Colletto directed at him and others. As the months passed, he felt that Colletto had broken his spirit: he became so despondent that he considered suicide. He quit the football team, and dropped out of school.

The lawsuit failed because his family did not have the resources to fight Purdue's powerful law firm in the courts, but Ryan believed that it had been worthwhile for him to expose abuse in college football. He and several players from other schools discussed mistreatment by their coaches on ESPN television. Ryan was convinced that his lawsuit forced Colletto to stop abusing players.

We pressed Ryan for more details, but he said it was too painful to discuss.

At this point, we believed we had done everything we could to verify the Tulane and Colletto claims. Materne's story about Davie's role in the spying incident was compelling and believable. The Colletto situation was more problematic. Was it a case of a player overreacting to Colletto's coaching style or had there been real abuse? And what did Bob Davie and Notre Dame know about Jim Colletto when they hired him? Given the extent of newspaper and television coverage of Harmon's lawsuit, we believed that they had to know about the allegations of abuse. It wasn't credible that they fire would Joe in part for abusing the player and then hire Colletto as his replacement.

Before filing the suit, we still had to see whether there was corroborating evidence of age statements by Davie—specifically, whether Davie made incriminating statements to the offensive line players after he fired Moore.

In mid-January, a month and a half after Joe was fired, Mimi drove from downtown Chicago, past the Gary steel plants, into the northern Indiana farmlands—a route she had taken many times during her four years at St. Mary's and on her trips to Notre Dame football games with her husband. After an hour on Interstate 80, the flat winter farmland evolved into a more rolling landscape. She passed the Knute Rockne Toll Plaza on her right—an indication she was nearing Notre Dame territory. After fifteen minutes, she left the tollway, heading down Route 31 past St. Mary's to the Notre Dame campus. She followed the handwritten directions, turning left at the Notre Dame golf course and then past the enormous stadium a few blocks to the Moores' condominium.

They were eagerly awaiting her. They had talked to her often on the telephone, but they had not yet met her. They were surprised to see this slight, dark-haired young woman in jeans and sweatshirt, looking more like a college freshman than a high-powered lawyer. When they were settled in the living room, they asked her about other cases the firm had handled and about her own legal experience. Finally Joe asked, "Why are *you* interviewing the players instead of Lieberman or Klenk?"

Mimi told them that she knew the scene at Notre Dame and also it was thought that the players would not find her intimidating and would relate to her.

"Well, I guess they would rather talk to you than Tim or Rick." Joe began to chuckle, struck by the idea of a waif interviewing the Notre Dame offensive line.

It was mid-afternoon and Joe and Fran began pressing food on Mimi. Joe insisted that she would need something to eat because it would take a while to track down players: "Fran, make her a Moore burger." This was a grilled ham and cheese sandwich.

While the three were together in the apartment kitchen, Mimi could not help but be aware of the Moores' special relationship. Fran was clearly an active partner in this enterprise; she knew a good deal about the school's football program, and was intensely involved in talk about the lawsuit. Occasionally, Joe would tell her good-naturedly to "shut up" so that Mimi could answer their questions, but he respected Fran's opinion, and deferred to her often. Mimi liked them both. They were obviously deadly serious about this lawsuit and were asking intelligent questions. They were also funny and warm.

Joe paced around the kitchen, never sitting down, as if he was involved in a pre-game planning session, while they worked out a strategy for approaching the players. They would first contact the senior players, who had had a longer relationship with Joe and were more likely to feel comfortable helping him. They hoped that after they talked to one or two of the players, the grapevine would spread the news, and all the players would know what was happening, and would decide that cooperating with Joe was "the right thing to do."

Joe and Mimi set out in late afternoon in his van, to see Jeremy Akers, the first name on his list. Akers was a fifth-year offensive guard—a star who had more playing time than any other Notre Dame player in that position. He had already earned a degree in economics with a 3.3 grade average, and had his teammates' respect. Joe parked in front of a dilapidated house in a rundown neighborhood near the campus, and he and Mimi left the van in the freezing cold; it seemed even colder to Mimi than the zero reading—she remembered South Bend as having an even more miserable winter than Chicago.

Akers met them at the door; Mimi, who knew a lot of Notre Dame athletes, was struck by his size: three-hundred pounds, six feet six inches tall. He seemed relaxed as he greeted Joe: "Hey, Coach, what's going on?" As they walked into the house, Joe said gruffly, "This is Mimi Moore. She's one of my lawyers and she's investigating my termination. She wants to find out what happened and she wants you to tell her the truth." Akers glanced at her, said, "Hey, Coach, you have to see this," and took Joe into another room to show him a school project he was working on. It looked as though Joe was a father figure for Akers.

After they came back, Mimi asked Akers if she could talk to him alone; they sat at the kitchen table while Joe waited in the other room. Akers said that in early December, Justin Hall, a graduate assistant coach, had told all the offensive line players to come to a 4:00 P.M. meeting with the head coach. Davie arrived about a half-hour late and told the entire group, "Joe and I sat down this morning and we believe the right thing for you guys is that I look for another offensive line coach. He is going to be sixty-five years old this February. Maybe he's going to coach for another year or two. I want a coach who will be here for five years so the recruits who are coming in will have a coach for their whole time. I want all the coaching changes to get over with right now. I don't know if this is going to come out as a firing or a retirement. I don't know how they are going to report this, but that's not important now. I want to do the best thing for you guys."

"Are you certain that Coach Davie mentioned Coach Moore's age?" Mimi asked.

"Yeah, he mentioned his age two or three times during the meeting." Akers said that immediately after the meeting, Davie met with most of the players individually. Later the players talked among themselves, surprised by the announcement. Some wondered whether health was the reason Joe was leaving. They considered Coach Moore "the best" and wondered who could possibly replace him. Akers emphasized to Mimi that Notre Dame had the best offensive line in the country. Then, two days later, Davie met again with the players, and this time he asked Akers to tell him exactly what Akers had heard him say at the first meeting. Akers told Davie what he was telling Mimi today. Akers said he thought the follow-up meeting was odd.

From Akers' house, Joe and Mimi went to another neglected dwelling, where she almost gagged on the smell of rotten meat. One of the three massive young men who lived there explained that the refrigerator had been turned off during the holiday break and the food had spoiled. Strangely, it seemed to Mimi that the three giants were intimidated by her. "Are you really a lawyer?" one asked respectfully. "Where do you work? Are you Coach Moore's lawyer?"

Mike Denvir, a senior offensive lineman, seemed particularly uneasy. Mimi was afraid that he would completely freeze up when she interviewed him. When they were alone, Mimi asked him what Davie had said at the players' meeting. Denvir paused. "He said he was looking for a younger coach." Denvir agreed to sign an affidavit which included his recollection that Davie said he wanted "young coaches with lots of energy," and that Davie specifically mentioned Coach Moore's age.

As the afternoon progressed, the players asked Mimi as many questions as she asked them. "What does this mean?" "Who could get in trouble for this?" "Can Coach Moore get his job back?" She replied that she was simply investigating and gathering facts. In the end, every player confirmed Davie's age statements, although each had a slightly different memory of precisely what he had said. All of them signed affidavits swearing to their recollections.

That evening, Joe and Fran took Mimi to dinner at an unpretentious Italian restaurant in Mishawaka, a town near South Bend. Everyone seemed to know Joe. People stopped at his table to say hello; others shouted "Hey, Coach!" across the room. Joe responded warmly; both he and Fran were talkative and friendly. Justin Hall, the graduate assistant coach who had worked with Joe on the offensive line, joined them for dinner. Afterward, at the Moores' apartment, the phone rang constantly with calls from friends all over the country. People phoned to talk about Joe's firing, about football, and just to gossip. Joe couldn't work the call-waiting apparatus, and kept passing the phone to Fran to do it.

That evening Mimi interviewed Justin Hall, who had missed the players' meeting and didn't know about Joe's termination until the next day when Davie came into his office and told him there were going to be changes on the offensive staff. Joe would no longer be the offensive line coach, Davie said; Joe planned to coach only another year or so and Davie wanted someone who would be there for at least four or five years. When Justin expressed surprise, Davie said, "Christ, let's face it, he's sixty-four years old."

Hall didn't believe that Joe was planning to retire in a year or two. He had worked with him every day over the past year and Joe had never given any indication that he was thinking about quitting. Hall knew also that Joe had recruited all of his players with a promise that he would be with them during their entire time at Notre Dame. Hall too signed an affidavit for Mimi.

She phoned me that evening, somewhat troubled that the players had inconsistent recollections of Davie's remarks at the meeting. I wasn't concerned; a jury would think it was contrived if the players had the same word-for-word memory. I told Mimi to continue getting signed affidavits. She said that Joe would be a good witness and a good client. His conduct was professional, and he followed her instructions to the letter about what he should say to the players.

The biggest surprise of Mimi's report was that the Notre Dame lawyers had not contacted the players. Since settlement negotiations had broken down, Notre Dame had to know that there was at least a possibility of a lawsuit—so I thought that they had not approached the players because they didn't want to put these students in the middle. If that were so, the school certainly wouldn't want to fight a lawsuit where the offensive line would testify for their former coach. I couldn't believe that any responsible university would permit this, and if it came to that, surely many parents would protest. But regardless of what happened, we had scored a major preemptive strike and, with signed affidavits, had locked in the Notre Dame offensive line for ourselves.

The following morning, Mimi and Joe left the condominium at seven o'clock to catch the younger players at their dorms. One player interviewed by Mimi that morning, Mike Rosenthal, made a particularly strong impression on her. Joe said that Mike was perhaps the best offensive guard in college football. Mimi waited in the dorm lobby while Joe went up to Rosenthal's room. Several minutes later, a disheveled young man appeared.

Even half-asleep, he was the perfect model of a Notre Dame football player—clean-cut, earnest and respectful. As Mimi and Rosenthal sat alone in the lobby, he told her, "I'd do anything for Coach Moore. I can't believe he's gone." Rosenthal said that when Moore recruited him, he promised he would always be his coach. Now, as a sophomore, with two years to play, Mike was extremely upset about losing Joe. The guys in his class, he said, were especially devastated by Coach Moore's departure.

Rosenthal's sentiments were reflected by the other players. Jeff Kilburg, whom Mimi talked to on the phone, said that although Coach Moore could be hard on the players and sometimes yelled at them, they all knew that his main concern was their welfare and that he was always pulling for them.

Every player interviewed by Mimi that day had heard about her meetings the previous day, and all were cooperative. They were all quite aware that they were helping Joe and hurting Davie. Some of them had detailed recollections of what had been said. Jon Spickelmier said Davie told the players he wanted to start the program over with younger coaches. Others had vaguer recollections, but all remembered that Davie talked about Coach Moore's departure in connection with his age. During the follow-up meeting with Davie, some players had told him that they believed he had described Joe's termination as a mutual decision or a "retirement." Davie corrected them, saying that he alone had made the decision.

After each interview, Joe anxiously asked Mimi, "How did it go? Are they for me or against me?" By the end of the day, she had nine signed affidavits, as well as interview notes from several other players who didn't want to sign anything. But she had not been able to contact Kaczenski, Clevenger and Doughty—three of the players who were slapped by Joe during the 1995 spring game.

As we worked on the case, we researched other potential legal claims that might increase the amount of our claim. If the case was for age discrimination only, the damages would be limited to back pay, front pay, and attorneys' fees. It seemed to us that Davie's statements to the players and others, also published in the *Blue and Gold Illustrated*, that at Joe's age he could expect to coach only another few years, were defamatory. In the same vein, the *Blue and Gold*'s editorial comment that Joe was physically incapable of putting in the long hours required of a college coach, appeared damaging to his prospects. We could not find any Indiana libel or slander cases involving derogatory comments about age or physical incapacity; but the statements did fit within the general Indiana definition of defamation as "words falsely uttered that directly tend to prejudice or injure a person in his profession or trade." Satisfied that a defamation claim had a sound legal basis, we now felt we could ask a jury for substantial damages.

We also discussed potential news coverage. We worried that right after we filed our lawsuit, a sophisticated Notre Dame public relations staff would destroy Joe in the media. Certainly, Notre Dame's powerful connections—including their NBC television contract and relationships with major sports writers—could have the impact of a nuclear bomb on our lawsuit. There were already signs that Notre Dame was preparing a media blitz. The January *Blue and Gold* article, suggesting that Joe was physically incapable of coaching, was probably a warning shot across our bow.

On the other hand, we were well aware that large organizations dread this kind of publicity. Increasingly over the previous five years, we received calls from our clients profoundly disturbed about possible high-visibility employment discrimination suits. Some of these companies settled for large amounts rather than risk headlines. While Notre Dame's apparently cavalier attitude toward settlement would seem to be an indication that they might not be worried about bad press, we believed that they were bluffing and that they were just as leery of publicity as any other organization.

I suggested that the best way to deal with this would be to hold a press conference when we filed our lawsuit so that we could get the jump on Notre Dame in the press.

Tim disagreed, saying that major press coverage of the filing would take away any incentive for Notre Dame to settle. "Notre Dame is hoping that no lawsuit will be filed. If we file the case without any publicity, it will send the message to them that we're serious about proceeding, and they'll be motivated to settle before the media picks it up. On the other hand, if we really hurt Notre Dame in the press, they could decide that the worst is over, and there wouldn't be any incentive for them to settle."

"But then," I said, "if we file the case with no publicity, Notre Dame may trash Joe in the press to discourage him from pursuing it. That seems to be their approach so far."

Ultimately, we decided that if we didn't take the offensive in the press, Notre Dame would probably do it. The question then became how to proceed. I envisioned having a press conference to announce the filing of the federal court complaint. But we had no contacts with the sports media and no experience with press conferences. In January, I telephoned Louise Edwards, a public relations sports specialist, and asked her whether the sports press would cover a press conference announcing the filing of this lawsuit. That, she said, would depend on what else was going on in the sports world at the time. "If it's a slow news period, I can get a decent turnout."

"Is this really a news story?"

"I think so, but we won't know for sure until we try. If Lou Holtz was bringing this case, no question about it. But Joe Moore isn't a national figure. If the press believes that Holtz has some involvement in this, it would help."

We came to an agreement, and Edwards said that she would tap every one of her connections to get coverage for our press conference.

Federal law requires that a charge be filed with the Equal Employment Opportunity Commission before a lawsuit can be brought. In late January we filed on Joe's behalf, including with the charge a request for a "right to sue" letter which would permit a lawsuit to be filed immediately. Even though the EEOC charge is not a matter of public record, we wanted to get the letter before word leaked out that we had begun legal proceedings. Under the EEOC rules, a copy of the charge is served on the respondent within ten days. We wondered if Notre Dame would contact us to resume settlement discussions before we went public, once they received a copy of the charge. But we heard nothing.

Several weeks after we filed, Joe got a phone call from David Haugh, a *South Bend Tribune* sportswriter, asking him to confirm that he was suing Notre Dame because of his termination. Joe referred him to me.

Haugh was one of several *Tribune* reporters who covered Notre Dame football. Joe said that Haugh was independent-minded when it came to discussing Notre Dame. Haugh phoned me the next day: "I understand that you're representing Joe in an action against the university," he said. I didn't want to answer this question. The disclosure that Joe was about to file would ruin our plan to create a big bang by announcing the lawsuit to the national media at a press conference. I asked if I could talk to him off the record, and he agreed.

"Look," I said, "we're bringing a major age discrimination and defamation case against Notre Dame over Joe's firing. We can't file the lawsuit until we go through the administrative steps with the EEOC and that should happen within thirty days. We'll probably have a press conference when we file the suit. If you hold off till then, I'll give you an exclusive beforehand."

"What kind of press conference do you have in mind?"

"We think this could be a national story and we're hoping we'll get major newspaper and television coverage of the conference. If you wait, you'll have an inside briefing on a big story; if you print something now, it probably won't make much of a splash."

Haugh paused. "If we could have a one-day jump on the story, maybe we could work out an arrangement. But I'll have to talk to my editor about it and get back to you."

I was heartened. He obviously agreed that the story would be more valuable to him if it was also covered by major newspapers and television.

Several days later, he called back. "I talked to my editor. He says we can wait to run our story until you file your lawsuit. By the way, have you done any investigation into Davie's background?"

"A little bit."

"You've obviously read about Davie's criminal indictment at Arizona. Do you know anything about Davie at Tulane?"

"I know something about Tulane, but if I share it with you, I want it to fall under the terms of our deal—that you don't publish anything you've gotten from us until the day before our news conference."

Haugh told me that he was already familiar with the details of the Tulane/Mississippi spying incident from newspaper files, but his investigation had reached a dead end. "I can't find the graduate assistant spy to see what he has to say about it. He disappeared from New Orleans years ago. Notre Dame's people told me that this guy was a wacko and Tulane only settled with him because the case was a nuisance. Davie says the guy's a nut who took his car without permission. He thinks the whole thing is ridiculous and he'll stand on his record. So at this point, I don't really have a story."

"Do you want his phone number?" I said.

During the three weeks after we filed the EEOC charge, Mimi repeatedly phoned the government office asking when the right-to-sue letter would be issued. Finally, an EEOC supervisor, tired of being badgered, told her that they would issue the letter in a few days. Now we had only a few days to complete the court complaint so it could be filed on the day of the press conference.

I wanted to hold the conference on February 25, but Louise Edwards, our public relations consultant, urged us to hold off for two more days because she would have more success getting media coverage later in the week. She was certain she could get some coverage, but wasn't sure how many reporters would come. We decided to hold the conference in the Ross & Hardies law library. I was afraid that we might get only four or five reporters so I decided to try to drum up more interest. I phoned Mike Sneed, a gossip columnist for the *Chicago Sun-Times* whom I knew, and told her about the case, hoping she would run an item in her column the day before the press conference. Naively, I didn't think an item in a gossip column would violate my pledge to Dave Haugh.

The following morning Sneed ran the item at the top of her column on the second page of the *Sun-Times*. It read, "A former football coach is planning to file a lawsuit against Notre Dame claiming age discrimination and defamation of character. Is there a scandal in the making?" Several hours after the paper hit the streets, Haugh called me, sounding upset. "Rick, I'm sorry but I can't wait until tomorrow to run the story. Someone must have leaked the story to the *Sun-Times* because there's an item in a column about it. We'll have to go with it tomorrow morning. It'll come out in my paper a few hours before your press conference."

Later that afternoon, my secretary ran into my office. She had just heard that CBS radio had reported that Lou Holtz was bringing a lawsuit against Notre Dame! Somebody had jumped to a hasty conclusion.

The morning of the conference, Louise, Joe, Fran, Mimi and I waited tensely in the Ross & Hardies conference room. Throughout my career I had tried to keep my clients away from the press; I had no experience in courting reporters. As for Joe, he had been in the limelight at Notre Dame for nine years, but this was different. Now he was about to announce that he was breaking ranks with Notre Dame and publicly airing a private dispute. He was upset. I tried to assure him that he had nothing to be nervous about; he had far more experience dealing with the press than anybody else in the room. The harsh reality of the undertaking was hitting Fran as well; she worried about the possible effect of all this on Joe.

At 1:30, we took an elevator down to the firm's 24th floor library, where a long table had been placed against a wall of books; the rest of the room had been cleared of furniture. As we walked in, I was stunned to find the large library filled, wall-to-wall, with television cameras, glaring lights, photographers and reporters. After we settled ourselves at the table, one of the reporters asked if we would wait for another television crew that was having parking problems. Louise Edwards whispered to me that there were reporters there from all four networks, and from ESPN, the Associated Press and both Chicago dailies. Everyone seemed deadly serious.

When they were ready, I said gravely, "Notre Dame's sixty-four-year-old offensive line coach Joe Moore is the best offensive line coach in the country, in either college football or the pros, according to Dick Vermeil of ABC Sports. In fact, almost every offensive line starter that Moore coached at Notre Dame has moved on to the NFL after graduation. Nevertheless, Moore was recently fired by Notre Dame's newly appointed head coach, Bob Davie, and, in a complaint filed with the United States District Court in South Bend, Indiana, Moore claims that Davie told him he was being fired because he was too old."

I gave details of our claims, including a request for three million dollars in compensatory damages for defamation. In an effort to blunt Notre Dame's expected defense, I said that statements that Joe was fired for abusive behavior and for not meeting university standards were false. I noted that Colletto had been hired despite his abusive behavior and that Davie's past was unsavory. As I spoke, bulbs flashed and intense television lights heated the room.

When I finished, Joe spoke, in his unpretentious rumbling voice. "I want to make clear that my nine years at Notre Dame, for myself and my family, are the best years I ever had in my life. I recruited almost all the offensive linemen that are still there and in recruiting them, I promised them I would be there for their career, particularly this year's senior group of Kaczenski, Doughty and Clevenger. I was with them when they were learning and now they're at a point where they will be great players. So you know it hurts. But Notre Dame still has been so good to me and my family, it's something I can't replace."

The reporters' questions were respectful. One asked, "What shape are you in, Coach? I mean, are you able to handle the physical demands of the job?"

"I was just down in South Carolina, and there were no golf carts and no pull carts, so I had to carry my bag for eighteen holes—I went around eighteen holes with no problem. Well, my stomach bothers me all the time, it's bothering me right now. But other than that, I don't know of any physical problems I have."

"Have you talked to Coach Holtz at all?"

"The last time I talked to Coach Holtz was the Sunday after the Southern Cal game and he thanked me for my service to him. He appreciated my contribution to his team and said that I was somebody very special to him."

"Joe, do you feel betrayed?"

"Well, I didn't know anything about the law or anything. When somebody tells you that you can only coach one, possibly two, more years and then they can't use you, it hurts you." Tears suddenly filled his eyes and he fought to regain control.

He'll be a great witness, I thought. He's sincere and honest, and these reporters seem to be eating out of his hand.

As the press conference began breaking up, one of the reporters, a young, good-looking, dark-haired man approached me, identified himself as David Haugh, and handed me a folded newspaper. "Let me know what you think. We'll be in touch," he said, and walked away.

Back on the 27th floor, we looked at the *South Bend Tribune* that Haugh had given me. A banner front-page headline announced the impending lawsuit, but what caught our attention immediately was a second lengthy article in the sports section headed, "Another Skeleton? Ex Coach Says Davie Helped Plot Spy Mission." Haugh gave details of Materne's story about the spying mission and cover-up at Tulane. Davie was quoted as saying, "I don't need to defend my position and my reputation. I'll take the high road."

Joe shook his head in disbelief, "This is going to destroy him."

As the Moores prepared to leave, Joe pulled me aside. "How does my case look?" he asked earnestly.

"It looks great," I replied.

That afternoon, I went home early to watch the five o'clock news. My seventeen-year-old son Todd was surprised to see me. I asked him to monitor one television, while I watched the other. "Hey, Dad, come here quick!" he shouted. On the screen, an announcer posed the general question of whether it is age discrimination to fire a college football coach when a new head coach is appointed. The screen image shifted to Joe, Fran, Mimi and me in the library; then to close-ups of Joe and me speaking, followed by a close-up of Joe's Notre Dame windbreaker and 1988 championship ring that Louise Edwards had insisted he wear. Todd, who had not shown much interest in the case before, said, "Very impressive, Dad. I think you're off to a good start."

Both the news conference and the AP wire story appeared throughout the country. All the reporting, including long articles in Chicago and Indiana newspapers, was sympathetic to Joe. Even the *Blue and Gold Illustrated*'s coverage provided only tepid support for Davie, noting that he had had the shortest honeymoon in Notre Dame football history: "The job is tough enough. Every man previously in Davie's position was judged by the results on the football field. Davie has yet to make it into the practice locker room."

Father William Beauchamp issued a written statement: "[The lawsuit] is entirely without merit, and the University will reply in the appropriate venue, which is through the legal process, not a news conference. Notre Dame has complete confidence in Bob Davie, a confidence which was a major factor in his selection as the University's new head football coach."

The following day when I called Haugh, he told me that the Notre Dame public relations office had complained to his editor about his reporting of the matter, particularly the Tulane incident. "Davie and Beauchamp apparently blew a gasket over these stories. They think I'm anti-Notre Dame."

"How is Notre Dame reacting to the lawsuit?" I asked.

"They're extremely upset about it. Joe has a lot of public support in South Bend. What I'm hearing is that the case should be settled."

He was convinced early on that Joe Moore's firing would become a major national story, and he was afraid that his paper might have to play catch-up with the national press in its own back yard. His editors encouraged him to spend as much time as necessary to develop the facts, and this despite Notre Dame's considerable power in the area.

I gave Haugh everything he wanted to know, but he was too good a newspaperman to rely exclusively on an advocate for one of the parties. He developed other sources, including someone in the Notre Dame administration. But the Notre Dame legal team refused to talk to him.

Ara Parseghian read the newspaper coverage of the lawsuit with a strong sense of foreboding. As one of the head coaches who had perpetuated the Notre Dame football legend for eleven years in the 1960s and '70s, he felt a deep personal responsibility to protect the university. He wanted Notre Dame's football program to remain the most respected in the world. But he also knew and respected Joe, and did not think he would launch such a high-profile attack against the university unless there was a good reason for it. He was particularly concerned that without an out-of-court settlement, an ugly situation would get even uglier. Seeing the early focus on the past conduct of Davie, Colletto and Moore himself, Parseghian was certain that this thing would turn into something like the O.J. Simpson trial with its airing of all kinds of dirty linen. He told Haugh, who telephoned him at his winter home in Florida, "Calmer heads should get together, sit down and work something out before it turns into that," meaning the Simpson case. "Before it's too late," he added.

Parseghian put out feelers to both sides, offering his services as a mediator. Since he knew everyone involved and was the revered elder statesman of Notre Dame football, he felt he was in a unique position to bring about a resolution. He spoke about it to Joe's close friend Tom Clements, a former

Notre Dame assistant coach and star quarterback, who called Joe with the offer. Joe, after talking to me, told Clements that he would be happy to have Parseghian try to work out a settlement. But we heard nothing further. The proposal never got off the ground.

IV

PRETRIAL LITIGATION

We decided that I would serve as lead litigation counsel; Mimi would be my second, and Tim Klenk would advise from the background, particularly on settlement. But there was no sign that Notre Dame had any interest in resolving the case. On the contrary, their approach was reminiscent of the Fighting Irish taking the field for a big game. They retained Barnes & Thornburg, one of Indiana's largest law firms. The lead counsel for them was to be Gerald Lutkus, a forty-four-year-old specialist in employment and media law. His team included John LaDue, a seasoned litigator for the firm, and two people from the school's Office of General Counsel: William Hoye, a senior litigator, and General Counsel Carol Kaesebier. This retention of four experienced lawyers seemed designed to send a strong message to us that the university intended to fight. Gerald Lutkus had earned both his undergraduate and law degrees from Notre Dame; for him, defending his alma mater would be a labor of love.

Within a few weeks after the filing of the lawsuit, Joe began to hear from friends that Notre Dame was aggressively investigating his past, contacting people who had known him as far back as his high school coaching days, over thirty years earlier. Chris Turner, Joe's former graduate assistant, telephoned Joe with the news that Davie himself had called Chris's uncle, Ron Turner, head coach at the University of Illinois, asking for Chris's phone number so that the Notre Dame lawyers could contact him. Davie added that Chris "better tell the truth because the lawyers know all about what Joe did to the players." Chris Turner told Joe not to worry: he had only positive things to say about him.

Mimi and I had several phone discussions with the Notre Dame lawyers to work out a schedule for depositions of witnesses and exchange of documents. The conversational exchanges were formal and polite. Lutkus said he would ask the court to limit the number of depositions that we could take, and implied that he was going to try to have portions of the case dismissed. Our earlier efforts to settle the case for a 1.3 million dollar offer was, he said, "ridiculous." When I asked him what their defense was going to be against our age discrimination claims, he answered that Notre Dame had opted not to renew Joe's five-year contract, and would not give their reasons for that decision until Davie testified at his deposition. I was somewhat surprised that four months after they had fired Joe, the university was unwilling to say why they had done it.

Soon after, Notre Dame filed a motion to dismiss the defamation claims against Davie in the complaint. They argued that these claims—that Davie made public statements that at sixty-five Moore was too old to coach and that Moore himself had said he could coach only another one or two years—failed as a valid claim of slander under Indiana law. I was fairly sure that the motion would be denied. Generally, federal courts are reluctant to dismiss claims based only on the pleadings. While courts will sometimes dismiss a case before trial based on a review of the evidence gathered during discovery, federal judges do not like to end a claim immediately after it is filed. However, we took the motion seriously: the defamation claim was important to us because it would enable the jury to award significant damages.

Judge Allen Sharp was assigned the case; on May 16, Mimi and I and all four Notre Dame lawyers appeared before him for the first time in the musty old United States District Court in South Bend.

Judge Sharp, a former Indiana country lawyer, had been appointed to the federal bench in 1973 by President Nixon. Considered to possess an excellent legal mind, he could be very tough on lawyers, and was sometimes unpleasant and unpredictable. Over the years, I had appeared in courts all over the country, and was used to dealing with difficult judges. Intelligence was the most important attribute in a judge, I believed. If Judge Sharp was a good legal scholar, I felt that we would be all right. I was pleased, too, to learn that he was sixty-five years old.

The judge began the hearing with a sardonic comment on the "celebrity nature" of the case. He asked Mimi and me to stand to be sworn into practice before his court, and went on to ask us where we had grown up, and where we had gone to college and to law school. I couldn't help feeling that he was aware that we were uncomfortable standing awkwardly in open court while he commented on our academic credentials. The judge then launched into a lengthy discussion of First Amendment media issues with Lutkus. Mimi and I listened in disbelief. We had no idea how freedom of the press could have any bearing on Davie's oral comments to the players and others not in the media. I was having difficulty even following the discussion.

The judge suddenly turned to me and asked curtly, "Are you relying on Illinois law here?" Mystified, I responded, "No, Your Honor. Indiana law." After only ten minutes in court, things already seemed to be slipping out of my control. Judge Sharp said that he saw this case as only age discrimination, not defamation. I disagreed with him.

"Words that tend to injure another in his trade or profession are defamatory under Indiana law," I said. "Davie's statements severely injured Moore in his profession, and therefore were defamatory as a matter of law. Davie effectively informed the football world that Joe Moore was at the end of his coaching career because he was sixty-five years old and therefore would only be able to coach another year or two. He drove the spike in even further by falsely stating that Moore himself had acknowledged that his coaching career was almost over when Davie claimed that Moore told him he could only coach one or two more years."

I argued that it was difficult to imagine any set of statements more devastating to someone's career than Davie's words about Moore—words that sent a message to the football world that Moore was washed up, finished as a coach, because of his age. "Why would any prospective employer ever consider hiring Moore as a football coach," I asked, "after his boss had publicly stated that age had diminished his abilities?" I brought up a federal appeals court decision in which a supervisor's comments that a sports reporter was no longer energetic enough to cover sports events, established a valid defamation case. Far more egregious was the public statement by Notre Dame's head coach that Moore was on a physical or mental downward slide, no longer able to coach football. A case like this, I said, should not be dismissed at this stage, before any evidence had been developed in discovery; the case should be allowed to proceed.

But the judge, unimpressed, reiterated his doubts about the defamation claim. He said he would consider the matter and issue a written opinion. Then he told us that the case would not be tried in South Bend, but in Lafayette in July, 1998. This would give the parties one year to take depositions and conduct other discovery.

Walking out of the courtroom, I whispered to Mimi, "He was only testing us. He won't throw out the defamation claims. Then, too, he's afraid of jury bias here in South Bend, and that's a good sign. This is a high profile case—he's going to be careful to avoid a reversal. He knows it would be too risky to throw out the defamation case."

Less than a month later, Judge Sharp issued a fourteen-page decision dismissing the defamation claim. In doing so, he had chosen to ignore the basic tenet that a claim should not be dismissed unless it appears beyond doubt that the plaintiff could not prove it. "What remains in this case is a rather standardized set of claims for age discrimination with celebrity parties involved," he wrote, concluding with the ominous comment that setting the trial date in July, 1998, "does not foreclose the defendants from challenging some or all of these age discrimination claims under Rule 56 of the Federal Rules of Civil Procedure, and no prejudgment on the issue is here intended."

Not only had Judge Sharp wiped out the possibility of our getting a large damage award (a decision that could not be appealed until all lower court proceedings were concluded), but he had issued an invitation to Notre Dame to later seek a summary judgment on the age claims which, if granted, would end the entire case before it ever got to a jury. Given his ruling on the defamation claim, anything was possible. This judge was fully capable of throwing out the entire case.

Newspapers across the country ran an AP story on the dismissal of the defamation claim. Father Beauchamp was quoted: "Today's ruling confirms the university's assertion from the outset of this litigation that the plaintiff's defamation claims against Coach Davie were without merit and that he never should have been named as a defendant in this case. As we continue to work through the legal process, we look forward to complete vindication on the remaining allegations against the university." I was quoted expressing disappointment with the ruling, and adding: "That is what appeals courts are for."

Shortly after this, the *Blue and Gold Illustrated* filed its own motion on the defamation claim against it, which was promptly granted. The *Blue and Gold* was dismissed from the case.

During the weeks following the rulings, we received many calls from friends and colleagues who said they heard that the Moore case had been thrown out of court. Our big successful press conference splash had been drained away. Now the public perception was that the entire case was over.

The pretrial discovery process in litigation involves exchange of documents and other information, as well as the opportunity to examine witnesses under oath before a court reporter. From the start, Notre Dame took a hard line. They turned down our routine request for the personnel files of all their assistant coaches. Since most of them were much younger than Joe, we wanted to examine the files for possible evidence that he had been treated differently from the others. If for example, the files reflected misconduct or job performance problems by younger coaches who were retained by Davie, it might establish that Joe was treated more harshly than they because of his age, or that he was not really fired for job performance. Generally, in age discrimination cases, the plaintiff is allowed to examine personnel files of younger employees who hold the same type of job. Courts consider personnel files to be relevant because they may provide evidence of different treatment between younger and older employees which can be used to prove or disprove a case.

When Notre Dame refused to turn over the files, we confidently filed a motion to compel production of the documents. Mimi and a young associate, Bill Wortel, drove to South Bend to present our arguments, but Judge Sharp was unsympathetic. He was more concerned about invading the privacy of the coaches than in evidence of age discrimination. Mimi pointed out that the files could be put under a protective order which would limit access to the lawyers and the parties, and protect the coaches' privacy. Judge Sharp said he would carefully consider the matter and rule later. He subsequently issued a short written decision denying our request for the files.

Joe and Fran decided that they needed to get on with their lives while they were waiting for the trial. In the spring of 1997, they sold their condominium and moved to Pittsburgh, where their sons lived. Joe began to look for a job. College coaching is a notoriously unstable profession, particularly for assistant coaches. It is not unusual for assistants to change jobs every two or three years. Joe had been fortunate to have a very stable career. He decided that at this point in his life, he was not going to take a temporary job where he and Fran would have to uproot themselves again after a year or two. Then, too, he was worried about Fran, who had been feeling fatigued and didn't know why. When her condition didn't improve, her doctor ordered tests, which revealed chronic emphysema. He prescribed medication and a portable oxygen machine.

Joe received several job overtures from struggling college teams. But he didn't pursue them because the tenure of the head coach at those colleges would probably be short. He interviewed for an offensive line coaching job at Cornell, which was in a substantially lower division than Notre Dame and the salary was less than half of what he had earned the previous year, but it was his best offer and he seriously considered it. He and Fran drove to Ithaca to look for housing. A secretary at the football office gave them a map along with the real estate section of the newspaper and sent them out alone. Fran was having a bad day with her emphysema. Driving in the unfamiliar city, they had trouble finding the addresses in the listings, and those they found were shabby and expensive. Frustrated and dispirited by the end of the day, they decided it was impossible. Joe turned Cornell down.

Fortunately, his friends came through for him. Kirk Ferentz, the offensive line coach of the NFL Baltimore Ravens, who had served as Joe's graduate assistant at Pittsburgh and greatly admired him, hired him as a consultant at $15,000 a year, to help train offensive line players and evaluate the draft potential of college senior offensive linemen. Joe was able to live in Pittsburgh and fly to Baltimore at the Ravens' expense. The Moores believed that Ferentz, a rising star in professional football, could move into a head coach job with an NFL team and bring Joe along as the offensive line coach. Joe also accepted a $30,000 part-time job with Tollgrade Communications as director of charities where, among other duties, he would plan and organize a celebrity golf tournament. Tollgrade gave him a $9,000 signing bonus as well. With these two jobs, Joe and Fran could get by until a stable coaching job came along.

I heard from a reporter about Notre Dame's defensive strategy: Joe was being characterized as someone who drank, was generally abusive and missed things in his work as a coach. There was going to be a big focus on his drinking habits, and the word was out that Davie had a major problem with Joe's abusiveness. In addition to hitting the three players during the spring 1995 game, there was another incident when Joe took a player's helmet off and hit him in the face. The bottom line was going to be that Davie had to get rid of Joe.

I knew about the spring 1995 game when Joe slapped several players during halftime. But I didn't know anything about any other abuse. And the drinking was news to me. When I asked Joe about this, he chortled. "Drinking? I might have one drink a week. I've never had a drinking problem. And I don't abuse kids. Tell me, how does my case look?"

We pushed forward with discovery, issuing subpoenas for files on Davie at Tulane and Arizona, and on Colletto at Purdue. When we got them, the Arizona file confirmed that Davie was one of a number of coaches caught in an expense account fraud conspiracy and subsequently indicted. The indictments were dropped after the head coach was acquitted. The Colletto file was basically limited to legal papers on the Ryan Harmon lawsuit. But the Tulane file contained new information.

Mimi and I were worried that the Gerald Materne spying affair might not be serious enough to help our case. But in the subpoenaed Tulane file, I found a letter from Grant Teaff, chairman of the Ethics Committee of the American Football Coaches Association, to Hindman Wall, Tulane's athletic director, asking for Wall's help with an investigation of the spying incident at Mississippi.

"As you are aware," Chairman Teaff wrote, "if these allegations were correct, it is considered, by our association, as extremely unethical; and it, of course, gives our profession, our association, and the game of football the kind of image that none of us want it to have."

In his turn, Wall assured the chairman that "Coach Materne acted entirely on his own in this matter without the knowledge and/or approval of either the head coach or any one of our other coaches," and he was terminated the day after the incident. Teaff answered that he was pleased with Tulane's prompt handling of the matter: "Unless further and different information surfaces, I am considering this incident closed."

Four months after the investigation closed, Hindman Wall, in a personal and confidential internal memo, told his superior, Tulane Senior Vice President Charles Knapp, that Materne had just informed him that "Coach Bob Davie had directed him to go to Mississippi State to spy on their team and provided him with $100 in cash and his car." The memo corroborated in every detail what Materne was to tell Mimi and me thirteen years later.

Wall also wrote Knapp that he intended to talk to Wally English and Davie to get their side of the story, and he did in fact write asking each of them for a written response to Materne's charges. Coach English sent Wall a memo declining to comment further and referring any inquiries to his attorney, Ned Kohnke. Davie also answered by memo: "Immediately after our initial conversation concerning the Gerry Materne case, I was prepared to give you a written account of the incident. As we had discussed, I sought legal advice concerning this situation. I was advised by my attorney, Ned Kohnke, not to issue a written account, as this could prove to be damaging to all concerned."

About a month later, in another internal memo, Knapp noted that Wally English had visited his office and "said that he had been aware that Coach Davie had sent Gerry Materne on the spying mission to Mississippi State. English said he had no prior knowledge of the incident." Knapp observed that this reflected a total change from English's original version of the incident.

The file also contained what appeared to be the handwritten instructions that Davie gave Materne to use on the spying mission.

I immediately telephoned the Tulane University lawyer who had sent me the subpoenaed files, and told him, "I think there are documents missing from the files."

"You have the complete file. I went through it myself."

"The American Coaches Association closed the investigation with the understanding that if any further information surfaced they wanted to know about it. But later Materne accused Davie and English of orchestrating and covering up the spying incident. Then English changed his story and said Davie was responsible for sending Materne to spy. Davie essentially took the Fifth and refused to talk, based on advice of his counsel. Are you saying that Tulane failed to contact the American Coaches Association to notify them that their head coach and one of their assistants were implicated in conduct that the Association considered to be extremely unethical?"

He hesitated. "Well, I know Tulane didn't go back to the American Coaches Association. Things had cooled down by then. Also, there was a question about English's veracity. He had been causing the university problems in other respects."

"Wasn't English's truthfulness a matter for the American Coaches Association to decide?"

"It's all water over the dam," he said impatiently.

The first deposition in the case was set for late July in South Bend. In a discrimination case, the plaintiff is usually deposed first, but we had quickly issued our notices of depositions before Notre Dame acted, so Davie was the first deponent in this case. I spent four long days preparing. Depositions are the most critical part of pretrial preparation; they provide a virtually unfettered opportunity for one side to learn the other side's case. When a witness gives deposition testimony under oath, he is locked into his story for the rest of the case. If he changes his testimony later at the trial, he will be impeached by his deposition testimony.

We decided to videotape the important depositions in the case. I had never done this, but I decided that now might be a good time to experiment with it, even though I wasn't sure exactly how we would use it.

The night before the deposition Joe, Mimi and I met for dinner at the Marriott Hotel in downtown South Bend. I wanted to know more about Davie and I asked Joe what he was like.

"He's always trying to figure out what's best for him. He makes friends with people he thinks can help him—everything is based on what will get him ahead. One time he asked me if I thought it would be a good idea if he converted to Catholicism. He thought it might help him get Holtz's job. That's how he thought. He made sure that Wadsworth, the athletic director, knew him so he would be in line for the job."

Mimi asked how Davie knew that Holtz would be leaving.

"He didn't, but it was pretty clear the administration was trying to drive Holtz out. They were all over him and it was probably affecting his coaching toward the end. It wasn't his fault. Wadsworth and the others just wanted him out of there and eventually he quit. Davie was getting ready to take a head coach position some place and he hoped the job would open up here."

"Why in the world would Notre Dame choose Davie when they could have had just about anybody they wanted?" I asked.

"Wadsworth and Beauchamp wanted someone they could control. Holtz was way too independent for them. He ran his own show and didn't listen to them. They wanted someone who was beholden to them. That's why they wouldn't take somebody like Barnett from Northwestern." Gary Barnett had just taken the perennial Big Ten loser, Northwestern, to the Rose Bowl and was the current shining star among college coaches. It had been widely reported that he was the top candidate for the Notre Dame job. "Barnett was just too strong for them. Wadsworth and Beauchamp think they can run the football program and don't need a coach with a proven record. They're probably right, because some years Notre Dame doesn't have a very tough schedule. This year, they could probably win eight games, and maybe more, with just about anyone coaching them."

The deposition was to take place in the conference room of our local counsel, Hammerschmidt, Amaral & Jones, a South Bend law firm. I had turned down Notre Dame's offer to conduct the deposition in their law offices; I wanted it on our own turf. We planned to meet Joe at Hammerschmidt's a few minutes before the deposition, but the streets around the building were closed off by the police and fire departments. We turned on the radio and heard that there was a gas leak in the center of town. I waited in the car while Mimi walked several blocks to the building where a policeman told her that it was closed for safety reasons. She searched the streets in vain for Joe, and finally came back to the car. It was now very late, and we assumed that the Notre Dame people would probably go to their Barnes & Thornburg law offices.

We rushed there frantically, and were escorted through elegant halls into a large conference room filled with expensive reproductions of eighteenth century furniture. Notre Dame had heard about the gas leak hours before, and had convened at their offices. Joe was somewhere in South Bend; we had no way to contact him. Perspiring and an hour late, we hurriedly unpacked our briefcases.

The room was crowded with six lawyers besides us: four for Notre Dame, and two representing the *Blue and Gold*: Kent Rowe of Rowe, Rowe & Maher, a crusty, veteran trial lawyer, and his associate, Marie Anne Hendrie. A court stenographer and a videographer were setting up their equipment. Davie introduced himself to Mimi and me. His hair was blow-dried and carefully styled, he wore a perfectly tailored blazer over a starched white button-down shirt and rep tie. I was struck with how cool and self-possessed he appeared, especially in contrast to everyone else in the room. As the eleven people took their places to start the deposition, the atmosphere was very tense. The demeanor of the Notre Dame team gave every indication that they considered this to be high stakes litigation.

Davie, sitting erect at the far end of the polished conference table, gave focused and controlled answers to all my questions. He had obviously been carefully prepared. He listened attentively to each question, and, after pausing, limited his response to that question, giving yes or no answers when they were appropriate, and volunteering nothing. He appeared completely unflappable

Davie testified that it was his sole responsibility to select assistant coaches and that no one else was involved in his decision to fire Moore. True, he had told the three-man committee that had named him head coach, which coaches he intended to keep, but he had not given them his reasons. I found it difficult to believe that this committee—comprised of Michael Wadsworth, Father Beauchamp and George Kelly, the assistant athletic director of football—would permit a young, inexperienced head coach to fire a long-time employee without any input from them. When I asked what, if anything, Davie knew about the application of age discrimination laws to hiring or firing coaches, he acknowledged that he had known that age discrimination laws applied to the employment of assistant coaches.

In response to my questions about the events of December 2nd, 1996, Davie's version differed markedly from Joe and Fran's. Davie testified that he told Joe, "This is probably the hardest thing I've ever had to do. I've known you for a long time. I've known you for twenty years, but I'm not going to be able to hire you. Let me tell you why." Before he could explain, he said, Joe jumped up, and interrupted him. "Bob, you don't have to tell me anything. I understand how this thing goes. This is your decision. You don't have any obligations to me. I was only going to coach another year or two anyhow." So, Davie went on, he felt that he owed his friend an explanation, and although he had many reasons for letting him go, he gave him the least hurtful one: Joe's often stated intention to retire in the near future. Davie explained to Joe that he had to have continuity in the coaching staff: "You know I want a five-year type plan, a five-year type commitment in fairness to these kids and in fairness to the program."

I asked him whether he had said, "At your age you have one, possibly two, more years to coach."

Davie denied that vehemently. "I never said that. *He* said that." Moore had told him many times that he intended to leave Notre Dame within a year or two, to go back to Pittsburgh and become a part-time coach at a high school or small college.

For months, we had speculated about how Notre Dame would respond to the Moores' claim that Davie fired Joe because he thought he was too old to last for the five years of Davie's contract. Now we knew. Davie was telling us that Joe had volunteered that he would be leaving in the next year or two, and that Davie, accepting that, had simply told him that such a short tenure would be inconsistent with his desire to have a long-term commitment from assistant coaches. It didn't sound like age discrimination at all, but rather like a normal action by a new head coach who wanted stability in his coaching staff.

Davie said that he expected no more of a commitment from Joe than from any other assistant coach. "My thought was I'm going to be judged—I've got a five-year contract. I

want to be judged over what happens over the long period
of time. I'm not going to be judged on the first game or the
first season. We had so much turnover among coaches, you
know, continuity was very important to me in hiring a staff.
I think it's been well-documented that there's probably not
been another university in the country that's had more
coaches, assistant coaches turnover, than Notre Dame in the
last several years." In order to eliminate that problem, Davie
said he needed to get "coaches that will stay."

I tried to get him to admit that he made age-related references when he talked to Joe: "During the meeting, did you
say that you needed a coach who was younger and who would
be around four or five years?"

He responded coolly. "I never said I needed a coach that
was younger, but I did probably say I wanted a coach that
was going to be around five years that could make that commitment to me."

"Did you say, 'I want young coaches with a lot of energy'?"

Looking at me as if I was having trouble understanding
him, he shook his head. "I didn't say that."

"Did you say he is going to be 'sixty-five years old this
February'?"

"I may have said that in the conversation. I'm not sure if
I did or not."

Davie stood up well to a barrage of questions about
whether he had made any age-biased remarks. But then I
moved on to a conversation he had had with Justin Hall, the
offensive line graduate assistant who worked with Joe. "And
is it correct you said to Hall, 'Let's face it, he's sixty-four
years old'?"

"I may have said that, " he said.

"Why did you say to Justin Hall, 'Let's face it, he's sixty-four years old'?"

He appeared to hesitate for a moment. "I don't know, other than it had come up in the conversation with Joe about when he was going to be—you know—was he sixty-four or sixty-five? I don't know why I would say that."

The only reason he would say that, I thought, was that it was the reason he fired Joe.

Joe came in and sat down at the back of the crammed conference room, just in time to hear Davie calmly explain his main reasons for the firing: "Well, the first thing I would say, would be physical and mental abuse towards the players. There were an awful lot of stories, but the things that I know happened were in spring '95. We had a spring game in the stadium, and we divided the teams up. It's supposed to be a fun situation, really, for everyone. It's kind of a reward for the players. I think the score was nothing-nothing at half time and Joe got the five offensive linemen into the locker room and went down and punched each one of the five. Several of them were left bleeding. The word spread throughout the entire team, and the entire coaching staff, really, before we ever left to take the field."

And, Davie testified, there were many other instances of Joe's physical and mental abuse of players. At the 1995 Florida State game, Joe punched two offensive linemen underneath their face masks. Just as an ABC cameraman was about to capture one of the assaults for a nationwide audience, a Disney executive, standing on the sidelines, rushed over and blocked the camera. At this past fall's Notre Dame-Navy game in Ireland, Joe punished players who were late for curfew by marching them to the hotel parking lot at one in the morning, and ordering them to do "up-downs," a brutal exercise where they run in place, dive into push-up position, bounce back up and then repeat the process. Guests in the hotel saw the incident from their rooms and consequently Notre Dame officials heard about it. Davie testified that he would not tolerate such abusive behavior by any member of his staff.

As Joe listened to Davie, he understood all too well that Notre Dame was now making good on Carol Kaesebier's threat that he would never get another coaching job if he brought a lawsuit.

Davie continued the litany of abusive conduct. Joe regularly made players perform "bear crawls," a punishment in which players are forced to go down on all fours and crawl back and forth over the practice field for thirty minutes. He misused the "mirror dodge drill"—where players dodge back and forth, mirroring one another—until the boys collapsed from exhaustion. Joe constantly shouted, verbally intimidating the players, calling them "pussies," "cowards" and worse.

In addition, Joe defied rules, smoking on the practice field despite NCAA policy, and in his office and during staff meetings, to the annoyance of the other coaches. He argued with Holtz in front of the players at practice. "If Lou wanted something done a certain way and Joe didn't agree with that, there would be open confrontation on the practice field of arguing back and forth." Joe also defied Holtz's authority during players' briefings, by frequently wandering off in the middle of meetings. Every morning at eleven, he left practice and did not return until a quarter of two in the afternoon.

He liked to hit golf balls behind the practice field while the other coaches were hard at work. He was the only coach who drove his car onto the practice field—too lazy to walk from the parking lot. He didn't change his clothes in the locker room after practice with the other coaches and left staff meetings before they were over. He routinely drank alcohol with underage players. His office was a disorganized mess with papers everywhere—once he even set his office trash can on fire. Davie was particularly appalled to see how filthy Joe made the car lent to him by a South Bend automobile dealer. The dealer eventually withdrew from the coach car loan program because Joe abused the car so badly that it could not be sold after he turned it in.

Addressing Joe's job performance, Davie said, "I didn't think our offensive line was particularly good."

"Why was that?"

"Watching us play, I think we got confused on who to block when people did something different. An example would probably be the Air Force game. There was a lot of confusion on who to block, is what I witnessed."

Davie said that Holtz shared that opinion. "So Lou felt frustrated that Joe either could not grasp or would not teach the blocking assignments and rules the way that Lou wanted them taught. After our last scrimmage in the spring of 1995, Holtz announced that he was going to coach the offensive tackles himself in '96. He said that the job had gotten too big for Joe and that's way too many guys for him to coach. Holtz said he would step in and coach the tackles." Holtz became increasingly frustrated with Joe during the past season. On one occasion, "Lou just snapped in the field and said 'We're not teaching them our rules.' He went to each offensive lineman and made them state his blocking rules."

During a break in the deposition, Mimi, Joe and I talked quietly in the hallway. Joe asked once again how his case looked. I told him that Davie was certainly well prepared and a lot smarter than I thought he would be.

"You think he's smart!" Joe said. "I don't think he's that smart."

Mimi said he reminded her of Bill Clinton.

"Clinton's smart," I pointed out.

Joe seemed depressed. "I have a long drive back to Erie. I'd like to start before it gets too late. Is it all right if I leave?"

"Absolutely, Joe. I'll call you tomorrow with a report on the rest of the deposition."

Notre Dame had launched a nuclear attack against Joe, and Davie had flawlessly delivered it. But I thought that they might have made some mistakes. Davie may have given too many reasons for firing Joe. It might look like overreach. And too, Davie's repeated references to Joe's defiance of authority opened the door for the court to consider Davie's misdeeds at Arizona and Tulane. How could Davie credibly claim that he fired Joe for defying authority, when Davie himself had a history of defying authority by defrauding the University of Arizona of expense account funds, sending an assistant coach to engage in criminal trespass at Tulane and orchestrating a cover-up to hide the truth from his superiors? If he was going to testify that he fired Joe in part for defying authority, then we could certainly introduce the Arizona and Tulane evidence to show that Davie had repeatedly done that himself. If a jury decided that Davie didn't really care about obeying authority, they might find that he wouldn't have fired an assistant coach for that reason and that he must be covering up his true reason—Joe's age.

I wanted to conclude the deposition from a position of strength by asking Davie about Arizona and Tulane. I proposed to the Notre Dame lawyers that we stop at five and reconvene the next day, but Lutkus balked. "Coach Davie is unavailable tomorrow. We gave him to you for one day, and he's much too busy to continue with this tomorrow or any other time."

I pointed out that the formal deposition notice required Davie to appear "day-to-day" until the deposition was completed.

"He's got a speaking engagement out of town tomorrow. He can't continue."

"Well, then, we need to call the court because he's obligated to continue this deposition until we finish. Let's get the judge on the phone."

They did not seem to like that; after they conferred privately for a few minutes, Lutkus suggested we work into the evening. The intensity of the day had given me a headache, and I wanted to stop. I looked at Davie; he still appeared fresh, but I couldn't believe that he wasn't wearing down. I decided that if Davie could do it, I could do it.

"Let's continue," I said.

I asked Davie about the hiring of Purdue Coach Jim Colletto, to show that Notre Dame hired him despite his well-known history of abusive behavior. Davie testified that before he was offered the Notre Dame job, he interviewed for the Purdue head coaching job to replace Colletto. The Purdue administration expressed great respect for Colletto and suggested that if Davie accepted the Purdue head coach job, he should consider keeping Colletto on the staff. Several months later, Davie, now Notre Dame's head coach, interviewed Colletto for the offensive line and coordinator jobs, was impressed with him and hired him.

"During the time you were interviewing him, were you aware of any alleged reputation that he was physically and verbally aggressive with his players at Purdue?"

"I did not know that, no, did not hear that."

"And during the time you interviewed him, were you aware of a lawsuit against him by a player named Ryan Harmon where Harmon alleged that Colletto physically hit, punched, kicked, and shoved with regularity as a method of coaching?"

"I was not aware of that, no."

"Did you see any newspaper articles in 1995 regarding Colletto's confrontation on the sidelines during a game with tailback Cory Rogers?"

"I had not seen that, no."

"And were you aware of an episode also reported in the press where Colletto allegedly threw a chair at player Steve Power in a locker room at the Northwestern game?"

"No."

"Did you get any information before you hired him about an ESPN program where one of his players was interviewed, and talked about how Colletto had beat him up, used swear words toward him, and physically and mentally abused him?"

"I've never seen that report, no."

"Did you ask him, 'Have you ever been accused of improper conduct with any other players at Purdue?'"

"I never asked him that."

Frustrated by my inability to show that Davie had any notice of Colletto's abusive history, I tried to get him to acknowledge that the nature of college football sometimes results in physical contact between players and coaches. "Isn't it true that some schools think it's acceptable for their coaches to engage in aggressive physical and verbal actions with their players, including touching them, yelling at them, using swear words?"

Davie skillfully deflected the question. "It's where you cross that line. Aggressive coaching is one thing. Punching a kid is something else."

Throughout the many hours of interrogation, Davie sat perfectly erect and answered each question without a trace of emotion. He was a defensive coordinator, I rationalized, and it was his job to be prepared for every attack that came his way. But I badly wanted to shake his composure. I asked about the 1980 Arizona criminal indictment. Davie calmly acknowledged that he had submitted false travel expenditures, but only on the instruction of his head coach to make up for other nonreimbursable expenditures. Later, all of the Arizona coaches were fired and Davie moved on to Pittsburgh as a graduate assistant coach. The head coach, Tony Maso, was tried and acquitted, and the charges against the other coaches, including Davie, were dropped. Even though he was cleared of the charges, Davie had paid back the money.

The Arizona episode was, he said, a youthful indiscretion. "I learned a valuable lesson at a young age—that you're responsible for your own actions. Just because someone tells you to do something doesn't necessarily mean it's right and you're accountable for your actions. This was a great lesson to me in life and I tried to take what was a negative when I was twenty-four years old and turn it into a positive. That's really why I paid the money back."

At 9:15 that night, after over ten hours of testimony, Notre Dame decided that they wanted to adjourn until 7:30 the next morning. Davie was still cool and unfazed. I had a raging headache. To make matters worse, after we left the law offices, Mimi reminded me that the hotel where we were staying was booked that night and we didn't have reservations anywhere else. She spent forty-five frantic minutes telephoning motels and finally found a cheap one with two vacancies, outside of town. For hours I lay on a hard bed in a spartan room, trying to block out the giggles of a group of junior high school girls staying at the motel for a baton twirling contest. I finally fell asleep about four in the morning.

At 6:30 A.M., in the motel lobby, amid the swarm of thirty noisy teenage girls setting off for their baton competition, Mimi and I ate the complementary breakfast of jelly doughnuts and instant coffee. I was exhausted. "If it's only to erase some of their smugness," I muttered, "we've got to shake up Davie this morning."

Back in the conference room, Davie was as fresh as he had been the previous day. I started with the Mississippi spying incident. He flatly denied that he or Head Coach Wally English had authorized the spying mission or had any responsibility for it. He said that Materne was simply a gung-ho junior coach who had launched the mission on his own because he wanted to make an impression on his superiors.

"I've never seen someone that had more of a burning desire to be a coach," Davie testified. "I mean, here's a guy that's got a family. He was the same age I was, twenty-six or twenty-seven years old, and he wanted to be a coach in the worst kind of a way." Materne, he said, had borrowed his car to go back to New Orleans to take care of his pesticide business, and Davie had no idea that he was embarking on a spying mission. When I showed Davie the handwritten instruction sheet that Materne claimed had been provided to him for the spying mission, Davie admitted that the sheet was in his handwriting, but it related only to an innocent routine scouting of Mississippi State. Davie said he had visited MSU in the spring of 1983 and 1984 to watch their open practice games.

"Was there anything wrong with Materne spying on a team during their practice?" I asked.

"To spy on a closed practice would be unethical, yes." He said he wholly agreed with the American Football Coaches Association that any coach who engaged in such conduct should be required to appear before the association before he could return to coaching.

Davie said that he remembered that in early 1994, Hindman Wall, the Tulane athletic director, had requested a written response to Materne's charges.

"Is it correct that you, in fact, refused to give him a written statement?" I asked.

"No."

"Is it correct, in fact, that you went out and hired a lawyer immediately?"

"No."

"Is it correct, in fact, that you and Mr. English both hired the same lawyer at that time?"

"No."

"Did you ever tell Wall that you would not give him a written account or statement regarding the Materne matter because it could prove damaging to all concerned?"

"I would never say that to Hindman Wall, the athletic director. That would not be my nature to do that."

I handed him the February 3, 1984, memo from "Bob Davie to Hindman Wall" in which Davie refused to provide a response to the Materne charges based on advice of his lawyer, Ned Kohnke, that it could be "damaging." Davie was flustered for the first time in the deposition. "I don't remember this. I do not remember this."

"Are you saying you did not send this memo, or you just haven't got a recollection of doing so?"

"I'm saying that I do not have a recollection of doing this."

"And if you were, in fact, telling the truth in the matter, there was no reason for you not to give him a written account of the incident?"

"That's true. That's why I don't remember this." Somewhat discomposed, he groped for an explanation. "I may have talked to Ned Kohnke and got advice from Ned Kohnke in an informal type situation."

"Would you have any explanation as to how this memo could be in the files of Tulane University?"

"I don't, no."

He admitted that he had heard, at the time, that his boss, Coach English, had accused him of sending Materne on the spying mission. "It seemed like I heard that, you know, at the end of the '84 season that Wally had said something to

Chuck Knapp that I had sent Gerry Materne to Mississippi State."

"Why would English say that about you?"

"I have no specific reason," Davie replied, adding, "but I know there's an awful lot of jealousy in this profession and that anything's possible."

Deciding to quit on a high note, I ended my examination.

Kent Rowe, the lawyer for the *Blue and Gold Illustrated*, had a few questions: "Well, Coach, you know, I wouldn't ask you this, but circumstances are such here that are beyond my control and I don't have any choice in the matter. And I'm going to ask you this question. Before I do, I've got to remind you that you're still under oath here."

Davie's expression was strained. "I understand that."

"The question is this: can you get me four tickets to the Southern Cal game? My sister is coming in with her family from Los Angeles."

"We're going to object to that question," Lutkus said, smiling for the first time in two days.

"You don't have to answer that on the record, but I'll be watching my mailbox," Rowe said. "Thanks a lot for coming to Notre Dame and coming to this deposition."

I talked to my thirteen-year-old daughter, Claire, and seventeen-year-old son, Todd, about the Moore lawsuit. I wanted them to understand that I was handling an important case, helping someone who had been wronged. And I wanted to show them that people can do things of consequence if they try.

We spent summer weekends at our beach cottage in Door County, a peninsula on Lake Michigan in northeast Wisconsin. In the mornings I bicycled through the woods to a small inland lake where I swam and then bicycled back. One Sunday morning in August, when I returned to the cottage after my swim, I was annoyed to find Claire sprawled on the couch reading, wasting a beautiful day. I started to tell her that, when, to my surprise, I saw that she was reading the Davie deposition transcript which I had left on the table. "Dad, I'm almost finished with it," she said. "I'll go outside as soon as I'm done."

"Well, what do you think of it, Claire?"

Knowing how deeply committed I was to the case, she hesitated. "Gee, Dad, I'm really not so sure that you have such a good case. Davie has an awful lot of good reasons for not keeping Mr. Moore."

Two days before his deposition, Joe met Mimi in South Bend to prepare for it. Sitting in the Hammerschmidt, Amaral & Jones conference room in downtown South Bend, they reviewed the December 2nd, 1996, termination conversation, the most important part of Joe's testimony: the entire case would be built upon the foundation of Davie's ageist comments to Joe.

When we had met with Joe nine months before, he had easily recited, verbatim, the events of that day. But when he began to rehearse the conversation in preparation for the deposition, he developed a severe case of stage fright. Over and over, Mimi asked him to repeat the conversation: "What did he say to you and what did you say to him?" Each time, Joe left something out, juxtaposed the order of the conversation, lost his place or asked Mimi to prompt him. The more they went over it, the worse it got. While there was no question that the conversation had taken place as Joe originally told it, the pressure of repeating it word for word was unnerving him. Mimi knew that if he testified like this at the deposition, Notre Dame would use the muddled testimony at trial to argue that he had either fabricated the story or didn't even remember what Davie said.

"Joe, you left out 'At your age, I won't be able to count on you for five years'," Mimi told him.

"Right, right. 'The way I see it, I won't be able to count on you for five years'."

"'At your age.' We can't leave that out."

"All right," Joe said, exasperated. "Let's start at the beginning and go through the whole thing again."

The four Notre Dame lawyers, Davie, Mimi, Joe and I convened again at the Barnes & Thornburg conference room for Joe's deposition. The *Blue and Gold* lawyers were not there because their client had been dismissed from the case. Mimi was visibly pregnant with her second child, and Davie walked over to her and started a conversation about family. She was surprised that he was so friendly. He really wants people to like him even when they're against him, she thought. It was also strange that Davie and his lawyers separated from one another when they were not at the conference table. Usually lawyers keep their clients close to them, but Davie wandered around by himself.

Joe had his impassive game face on, but Mimi knew he was terrified. Lutkus began the examination. Referring to December 2nd, he asked, "And what did Coach Davie say to you?" Joe began a halting answer and then stopped altogether. Mute, he glared at Davie, sitting at the far end of the table, whispering to William Hoye. "He's interrupting!" Joe barked. "With them moving and talking back there, it's getting to my train of thought."

When he started again, he couldn't remember where he had left off, and the record was read back by the court reporter. He commenced again, carefully detailing the conversation in the proper order, but stopped again after another few sentences. There was a long pause. Mimi, whose heart had been thumping since he started, felt a wave of nausea. This is a nightmare, she thought. I'm going to throw up if he forgets.

Abruptly, as if galvanized by the danger of his situation, Joe flawlessly related the rest of the conversation. Mimi glanced over at the Notre Dame lawyers, who appeared to be unaware of the perilous straits that Joe had just navigated. We got through this, she thought, so we can get through anything in this case.

Many of Lutkus's questions to Joe had no bearing on the case, but were raised for the purpose of sending a message that Notre Dame intended to hurt him in any way they could. He relentlessly interrogated Joe about a 1966 incident when he had come to blows with another high school coach over some long-forgotten dispute, and a 1965 altercation when a referee hit Joe in the back of the head with a flag and Joe responded by knocking him on the top of his skull. Notre Dame had obviously dug deeply into Joe's life. That such incidents would not be admissible at trial, since they were not among Davie's claimed reasons for the termination, did not deter Lutkus from hammering away at Joe.

Any remaining fears that Notre Dame's strategy was to make the Moores so miserable that they would drop the lawsuit, were dispelled when Fran was deposed in Pittsburgh. Because of her emphysema, she had to bring a canister of oxygen with her to the conference room.

"Now, you have sons, correct?" Lutkus asked.

Fran acknowledged that she had three grown sons.

"Did you ever see Joe strike your sons in the face like he hit those players?"

"Objection!" I cried, shaking my head in disbelief. "That is totally inappropriate."

"I'm glad you find it laughable," Lutkus replied.

"I really find it to be desperation on your part to get into family matters."

Lutkus smiled. "This is a guy with a violence problem who hits his players. I want to see if there's a history of it."

With dignity, Fran interjected, "I have never seen him strike our children across the face."

"Do you think it is appropriate for a college football coach to strike his players in the face with his hands?"

"It is irrelevant, totally irrelevant," I said. "You are getting into an area which I think is blatant harassment."

Lutkus leaned back in his chair. "I disagree. I disagree."

"There's absolutely no way this would get into the court! It's opinion testimony by somebody who is not even part of the football team."

Undeterred, he began an inquiry into private conversations between Fran and Joe. Citing the marital privilege, I told her not to answer. Discussions between husband and wife are sacrosanct, I pointed out, and may not be brought into legal actions. But Lutkus continued to ask about these conversations, threatening to go to the judge to reopen the deposition and ask for court costs if she refused to answer. I instructed her not to say a word on the subject.

After the deposition, Fran, still furious, said that she believed that the university officials had told the lawyers to invade her privacy and humiliate her. But far from being discouraged, she was now more resolute than ever. She had taken a strong dislike to Lutkus and Hoye.

Lutkus never pursued my marital privilege objection with the court.

I still didn't believe that Davie had fired Joe without the involvement of his superiors. But when I deposed Notre Dame's athletic director Michael Wadsworth and Wadsworth's superior, Father William Beauchamp, I wasn't able to develop any evidence of their participation.

Wadsworth was a huge, imposing man who had once been Canadian ambassador to Ireland. Eventually, after some lengthy monologues, he testified that a committee comprised of himself, Father Beauchamp and assistant athletic director George Kelly, had selected Davie as Holtz's successor after rejecting Gary Barnett, Northwestern's superstar coach who was also in the running. The committee knew nothing at the time about Davie's Arizona indictment or the lawsuit against him at Tulane, but Wadsworth now said he was confident that Davie had not been involved in any impropriety at Tulane and had simply been following instructions at Arizona.

Wadsworth further testified that Davie, as the new head coach, had the unfettered right to select his own assistant coaches, and had simply informed the committee that he intended to terminate Moore and Earl Mosley, telling them that Moore was a lackluster recruiter and that Davie "had to have somebody who's going to be able to be one hundred percent into recruiting when required."

I nudged Mimi sitting next to me at the table, held my legal pad in front of our faces so the opposing lawyers couldn't read my lips, and excitedly whispered, "Davie testified about a million reasons why he fired Joe, but recruiting was not one of them. These guys didn't coordinate their story." Mimi nodded. She had already noticed that Wadsworth's testimony was inconsistent with Davie's.

Later that day, Father Beauchamp repeated Wadsworth's assertion that Moore was fired because he was a poor recruiter.

In late summer of 1997, before the start of the football season, the sports press described Notre Dame's new head coach in glowing terms. There was a six-page color feature in *Sports Illustrated* on Davie's high school record as a baseball, basketball and football star and his courtship of his future wife, JoAnne, a popular majorette; the photogenic couple later produced two beautiful children. Davie had received a football scholarship to Arizona, and risen through the assistant coaching ranks at Pittsburgh, Arizona, Texas A&M and, finally, Notre Dame.

A *Chicago Tribune* article, "Right Where He Belongs," compared his appearance favorably with Clint Eastwood's: Davie, the reporter said, was younger, taller and more handsome then the movie star and, with his clean-cut good looks, positive attitude and innovative ideas, was the right man to lead Notre Dame into another era of football dominance.

In another article, Lou Holtz was quoted as saying, "I believe the players will react very favorably to Bob. Bob is young, he's enthusiastic, he's a players' coach, and I think that's what Notre Dame needs right now. I'm more of a disciplinarian, and that's not what they need anymore."

The new look for Notre Dame football would be most apparent in the updating of the offensive line strategy which, according to *Sports Illustrated*, would "look like 1997 instead of 1965." Davie intended to move away from Notre Dame's traditional ground game where the offense simply crushed the opposition—running the ball protected by massive offensive linesmen. Davie's up-to-date offense, implemented by Jim Colletto, would employ a complex assortment of passing and running plays. Led by its glamorous young coach, the freshly minted Notre Dame would create excitement as well as victories.

"We're going to play to win, not prepare to lose," Davie announced. While the Moore lawsuit was not even mentioned by *Sports Illustrated*, the *Chicago Tribune* gave the impression that it was a frivolous, unfair attack, quoting Davie: "Everywhere I went, I was the clean-cut guy, the reliable guy. Then, all of a sudden I had to defend myself. I was disappointed but not shocked. I realize the magnitude of this job."

Mimi went with her husband and two friends to Notre Dame's opening game against Georgia Tech. She had been an avid fan when she was at St. Mary's and of course her devotion did not lessen when she married a former Notre Dame football team student manager. The two of them had cheered the team at many games. But now, as she entered the new 80,000-seat concrete stadium on this pleasantly warm September afternoon, her feelings were mixed.

Seated close to the Notre Dame sideline, Mimi had a good view of the field and of the stands, brimming with young college students, thousands of alumni of all ages and other enthusiastic Notre Dame supporters. It seemed that everyone was wearing Fighting Irish icons. Notre Dame was a heavy favorite, ranked in the top ten by the pre-season polls. Georgia Tech, on the other hand, was considered mediocre at best, rated in the mid-20s or below. As Davie and his squad of players in their stunning blue and gold uniforms came running out of the tunnel, the 80,000 fans roared their approval; they believed they were going to witness history in the making: the dawn of a great new era for Notre Dame football.

But from the moment the game started, something seemed to have gone very wrong. The Notre Dame team looked clumsy and tentative. Mimi's husband and their friend, who had also been a football student manager, exchanged nervous glances. "My God," her husband muttered, "they look terrible!" He didn't share Mimi's new ambivalence about the team, but was still an ardent fan. He could see that the new pass plays were not working, and neither was the team's usual ability to move the ball on the ground. As Georgia

Tech took the lead and held it, the stands got quieter and
quieter. Mimi was close enough to watch Davie on the sidelines. He had looked supremely confident at the outset, but
as the game progressed, he began to pace back and forth,
not talking much with the other coaches and players. In the
fourth quarter, Notre Dame made a touchdown and won,
17 to 13.

That evening Joe phoned Mimi at home. "They looked
like a high school team," he said, with his gruff chuckle.
"I've never seen them play like that. I can't wait to see what
happens next. How does my case look?"

Earl Mosley, assistant football coach in charge of run-
ning backs at Stanford University, was also watching Notre
Dame closely. Mosley's interest was both professional—
Stanford was scheduled to play Notre Dame in the middle of
the season—and personal: Mosley and Joe had been fired by
Davie at the same time.

Mosley, an African-American, had had a difficult five
years at Notre Dame. He was married to an FBI agent stationed in Chicago, where she had to maintain a residence
with their two young children, while his job necessitated his
living in South Bend. Mosley felt that the Notre Dame administration disapproved of this split-family situation. A
devoutly religious Christian, he tried hard to get along with
all of his fellow coaches, but most of them were unrespon-
sive, including Bob Davie, who was then defensive coordinator.

One of the few coaches who did befriend Mosley was
Joe Moore, who had recruited Mosley from Temple, strongly

recommending him to Lou Holtz. Mosley lived in the same apartment complex as the Moores, and had great respect for Joe as a warm person and a great coach who genuinely cared for his players and worked to make them into outstanding athletes and decent men. Moreover, Joe and Fran went out of their way to sympathize with Mosley's difficult situation.

A month before Mosley and Moore were fired, Notre Dame played Boston College in Chestnut Hill, Massachusetts. At the end of the first half, as Mosley was going into the underground tunnel leading to the locker rooms, someone in the stands above spat on him and screamed a racial epithet. When Mosley began to shout back, Lou Holtz rushed over and struck him; then several people grabbed Mosley and pulled him into the tunnel.

Earl Mosley was shocked by what Holtz had done. He complained to the Notre Dame administration, including Wadsworth, that he had been attacked by his own head coach. No one seemed interested. He had always behaved toward his colleagues with professional courtesy and respect. He couldn't understand how he could be treated like that, and he couldn't stop obsessing about it.

In late November, shortly before Holtz announced his resignation, Mosley and Davie were dressing for practice at their adjoining lockers. Davie leaned close to Mosley and asked, "Say, Earl, do you know how old Coach Moore is?"

"I think he's sixty-four, sixty-five."

"Hmm," Davie murmured. Then he asked, "You know how long he's going to coach?"

"I don't know. Coach Moore is a football coach, he'll coach forever in the right situation."

"What about you, how old are you?"

Mosley told him he was forty-nine.

The following week, in a private hotel dining room near the University of Southern California campus, Mosley was sitting with Davie and several other coaches and administrators. George Kelly asked him to move to another table for a private talk, and confided to him that he didn't know what was going to happen, but he wanted Mosley to know that Notre Dame cared about him and his family. "If things don't work out here, we'll help you get a job in the Chicago area," Kelly assured him. "What do you want to do in the future?"

"George, I'm a football coach and that's what I plan to do."

"Well, how old are you now?"

"I'm forty-nine."

"You know, you can't coach much longer."

Mosley was offended. "George, I'm a football coach! I mean, that's what God blessed me to do. And that's what I want to do."

Kelly said, "You know, you could get a job in athletic administration. I enjoy that very much."

"No, I'm a football coach." Mosley walked back to his table.

Several days later, after they returned to South Bend, and Davie's appointment as head coach was announced, Davie came into Mosley's office and told him, "Earl, I saw that you talked to George Kelly. I'm not gonna be able to rehire you as a member of my staff. I'm really looking for people just like me to be on the coaching staff."

The following fall, Mosley looked back on his unhappy time at Notre Dame, and decided that things had worked out for the best. The coaches at Stanford were honorable men, the head coach was an African-American, and he could not help feeling a certain grim satisfaction at Notre Dame's performance that fall. After barely beating the weak Georgia Tech team in the opening game, Notre Dame lost to everyone. They were defeated 28 to 17 by Purdue, the perennially low-rated team that Jim Colletto had coached, then by Michigan State and after that by the University of Michigan.

In late September, Joe and Mosley talked on the phone for the first time since they had left Notre Dame. They discussed the team's poor performance under Davie, and entertained the possibility that lower-ranked Stanford had a chance against them. Before they hung up, Mosley asked Joe how his lawsuit was going; Joe told him that it was in the hands of his lawyers. Mosley said, "I don't know if this means anything," and then told him what Davie and Kelly had said about age. Joe said he would pass the information on to his lawyers, if it was all right with Mosley.

To us, Earl Mosley's evidence was a ray of sunshine piercing black clouds. Davie's questions to Mosley about Joe's age and plans, showed that Davie thought that Joe was going to give up coaching in the near future because he was in his middle sixties. It was strong evidence of age discrimination that Davie had fired Joe despite being told by Mosley that Joe planned to coach forever. We quickly subpoenaed Mosley and videotaped his testimony. Notre Dame sent John LaDue, the most junior lawyer on their legal team, to the deposition: it would appear that they didn't consider Mosley's testimony important.

Notre Dame was defeated 33 to 15—its fourth consecutive loss—by low-rated Stanford, which overpowered Notre Dame in rushing—a traditional Fighting Irish strength. The sports media had a field day with the worst Notre Dame season since before the Holtz and Moore era; article after article dissected the team's unexpected slide.

Jim Colletto, the new line coach, received the brunt of the criticism. How could the heart of the Notre Dame team—the offensive line of experienced, six-foot-seven-inch, 310-pound mountain men who had dominated college football—perform so poorly? Colletto reached his nadir when Purdue, the team he had coached season after season, with results that were mediocre or worse, easily beat Notre Dame. He became an object of ridicule. One reporter noted sarcastically, "Jim Colletto finally figures out how to stop the Notre Dame offense." When Colletto said, "I don't hardly watch the game when calling the plays," one writer observed that if he did, "he might get mustard on his shirtsleeve."

Notre Dame fans, who had always been staunchly loyal, even through bad times, began to turn on the team and its coaches. After the University of Southern California handed Notre Dame its fifth loss in seven games, the Fighting Irish fans booed their own team as it left the field. Davie, trying to deflect criticism from the coaching staff, told the press that the fault lay with the players: the team was "discombobulated." He didn't attempt to explain why the same offensive line players who had performed so well the previous year, ranking eighth in the nation, were now un-

able to perform competently against even the weakest opponents.

I hoped that the stark reality of Notre Dame football
players being subpoenaed and deposed, would push the university into settling the case. Joe heard that player morale
had been devastated by the losses. I thought that Notre Dame
would surely want to keep their players out of a lawsuit where
they would have to take sides for or against their own head
coach. But my hopes were dashed by Judge Sharp at a conference to discuss the scope of discovery.

He asked us to talk about the players we wanted to depose.

Mimi told him these were the players who had been at
the December 2, 1996, meeting where Bob Davie had announced that Joe Moore would not be returning.

"How many are we talking about?"

"I believe there are eleven."

He looked at her with raised eyebrows. "And you're
wanting to take all of them!" he said.

She tried to salvage the situation. "We're expecting that
some of them may only take an hour."

The judge shook his head, leaned toward her and said,
"I'll tell you what you're going to get to do. You take your
best shot with two from that category and then you show
me why you need more than two players that attended that
meeting. Fair enough?" Somehow I had the feeling that he
wasn't going to accept our argument.

Gone was my hope that the involvement of Notre Dame's
entire offensive line in the lawsuit would provoke settlement,
and not only that, but now I was afraid that deposing only

two players might hurt our case. True, we had a stack of affidavits from the players, but affidavits are not admissible in court. To prove that Davie made age comments at the meeting, we needed live witnesses or videotaped depositions. We couldn't subpoena players to testify if they weren't within the hundred-mile federal court subpoena range, and if they weren't in South Bend during the July, 1998, trial, they would probably be beyond the range. In any event, I thought that calling the players as live witnesses at trial was too risky—they might say anything. Our best shot was to get lucid and compelling videotape testimony from the two players whom we were permitted to depose.

We debated endlessly which two players to choose. Each player had a different recollection of the December 2 meeting; some would make more compelling witnesses than others. We eventually settled on Mike Rosenthal, the clean-cut star of the offensive line who had impressed Mimi as honest and unbending, and Jon Spickelmier, the player who remembered Davie saying that he wanted a younger coaching staff. Rosenthal had been ranked by *Lindys*, a leading football magazine, as the number one offensive guard in college football.

The depositions were held in late September on the Notre Dame campus in the modern Center for Continuing Education building. I wanted Mimi to take the depositions because she had done so well with the players when she interviewed them, but she was late into her pregnancy and her doctor wouldn't let her travel. I went with my associate Bill Wortel, and with Joe.

When Gerald Lutkus and William Hoye entered the conference room, I was surprised to see that Davie was not with them. Mike Rosenthal had come with his father. As the video equipment was being set up, the Rosenthals chatted amicably in a corner with Joe, whom they were clearly delighted to see again. Mr. Rosenthal told me, "Everyone here has counsel except my son. That's why I'm here—to protect him."

We all sat around the big conference table, and I began to question Mike. I was concerned about making him nervous, but it was soon clear that I had nothing to worry about. He was the ideal witness—articulate and polite, and on top of that, he looked like a model for an Adidas ad. He testified that, at the December 2nd meeting, Davie discussed Moore's age and said he was terminating him because he wanted continuity in the staff: coaches who would be there for five years.

"I was kind of in a state of shock. I really didn't anticipate this meeting being that way. Coach Moore made a promise to us our freshman year that he was going to stay through our four years. He told me how he would coach me and what he would get me to do as a football player and as a person. He gave me a commitment from him that he would be there for me."

"Did he do that for you?" I asked.

"Aside from my parents, he's the single person that influenced me the most. He made me into what I am today, especially on the football field and in the classroom. The goals and the drive that he instilled in me were just incredible."

"And did you ever see Coach Moore physically or mentally abusing any football players?"

"No, sir. I saw him coaching to the best of his abilities and getting people to perform to the best of their abilities and driving them to do that. I think Coach Moore was such a great offensive line coach that I still had a lot to learn from him and in my two years I just didn't learn enough. I think he could have helped everyone just by coaching there and being there and, you know, being our offensive line coach." He added, "On the other hand, we do have a good offensive line coach in Coach Colletto."

I was pleased with Mike Rosenthal's testimony, but I hoped that Jon Spickelmier would provide more detail about Davie's comments at that December meeting. Spickelmier arrived alone, looking unhappy, and took his seat at the table. Clearly uncomfortable with being deposed, hesitant and stammering, he testified that Davie had told the offensive line players that he wanted "a young coaching staff that he could grow with." This was the testimony that I wanted: the desire for a younger staff was strong evidence of age bias.

But when Spickelmier was questioned by Gerald Lutkus, he began to waver, and implied that Mimi had intimidated him by writing out a statement for him to sign. I tried to salvage the situation by showing him his statement and asking him if he had signed it, and if it was true, as he had said, that Davie had said that he wanted to start the program over with younger coaches. Spickelmier replied, "He said that—he said that, but he said he wanted a—a con—a continuity with the coaching—with his coaching staff."

On recross examination, Lutkus asked him, "Jon, let me follow up on that. Do you recall Coach Davie saying he wanted to start the program over with younger coaches, or was this—were you—?" Spickelmier said, "I just remember him saying that he wanted a continuity," and then went on, without any prodding, to volunteer, "That's the words that I recall. I don't like—I don't remember anything about—anything about younger, but, I mean, it seems like that's—that's the—that's like—I put that—I put that down here, and I wasn't—I wasn't for—for sure. I mean, I don't know, but to tell you the truth, I don't remember him mentioning anything about having younger coaches . . ."

Attempting to salvage something from the massive player's testimony, I asked, "Did he mention Coach Moore's age in any way?"

Spickelmier, now confident, firmly replied, "No, he did not."

After the deposition, as we walked through the parking lot, I told Joe, "Well, we got one useful deposition out of this. I really wish we had more player depositions, particularly since Davie was so explicit in his age comments at that meeting."

"Tell me, Rick," Joe asked earnestly, "how does my case look?"

In the light of Judge Sharp's two-player deposition limit, we were surprised to receive a copy of a subpoena issued by Notre Dame to another player, Rick Kaczenski. When I phoned Joe with the news, he reminded me that Kaczenski was one of the players he had slapped in the locker room during the game in spring, 1995. Since we hadn't spoken to Kaczenski, I tried repeatedly to reach him in South Bend, but he was never home. Every time I called, his roommate told me that Rick was out shopping, out visiting his girlfriend or just "out." I obsessively telephoned at all times of the day and night for one solid week. Finally, late on Saturday afternoon, several days before the deposition, he an-

swered the phone. Introducing myself as Coach Moore's lawyer, I said "Look, I want you to understand that it was not
our idea to bring you into this. That subpoena is from the
Notre Dame lawyers."

Bitterly, he said, "I'm so pissed off at them for dragging
me into this. First they call me in last January and ask me a
bunch of questions. I thought that was the end of it. Now,
while I'm still playing football, they want more from me. I
mean, to be bothered by this during the season, it's just unreal."

"You know what they want, don't you?" I said. "They
want you to testify that Coach Moore abused you. He knows
it was wrong to slap you guys in the locker room, and he's
regretted it ever since. But they want to make more of it than
it is. They're saying Moore struck you guys with an open
fist. Now, when you testify, you should tell the truth. That's
what the coach wants. He remembers that it was a slap, but
I want to emphasize, we want you to tell the truth."

"The truth is that Coach Moore was the most important
influence for me at Notre Dame and they're assholes for putting me in the middle of this."

I called Joe at home that evening to tell him that I thought
Kaczenski was going to help us, and that we were not going
to try to quash the subpoena.

When Bill Wortel, Joe and I arrived for the Kaczenski
deposition at the campus, Davie was there with Lutkus and
Hoye. As we waited in the lobby for Kaczenski, Davie strolled
over to us, introduced himself to Bill and remained to chat
amiably as if he were relaxing with his best friends. His lawyers didn't seem to mind his consorting with the enemy.

Kaczenski, in a torn white t-shirt, looking as if he just left the set of *A Streetcar Named Desire*, arrived ten minutes late. We learned later that a campus police car had picked him up at his apartment and driven him to the deposition. But if Lutkus expected this player to be helpful to the university, he was doomed to disappointment.

Kaczenski said that as a senior in high school, he had been heavily recruited by many major football programs. He decided to visit Notre Dame because of the reputations of Lou Holtz and Joe Moore. When he saw the campus, he was simply overwhelmed.

"You see the Grotto, you see the Dome and it's just unreal. You know, I'm a senior in high school, and I'm talking to guys I've been watching on TV for three or four years. I was sold on the prestige, academics and football."

But life at Notre Dame turned out to be difficult. He struggled with poor grades; he disliked the other students, hated the social life and felt uncertain about his athletic abilities. He began to dread practices and games and seriously considered transferring to another university where the pressure would be less intense. When he confided in other players, he was surprised to learn that there were at least thirty others on the team who felt the same way. They had all had good high school experiences and were now insecure and unhappy.

At the spring games in his sophomore year, Kaczenski felt that he couldn't do anything right. The defense was crushing the offensive line and during the last play of the first half the line completely disintegrated, resulting in the sacking of the quarterback. At halftime in the locker room, Coach

Moore lost it. He shouted at the five linemen sitting on the locker room bench that they didn't deserve to be at Notre Dame. "You've got to get going!" he yelled, and slapped each one on the side of the face.

Kaczenski decided to quit school. It wasn't because of the locker room incident; it was his poor playing and general misery. But Coaches Moore and Holtz had more confidence in him than he had in himself. When he went home to Erie, Pennsylvania, both coaches visited him separately, asking him not to quit the program.

"I want to know exactly how you feel," Coach Moore said, and Kaczenski opened up to him as if Joe were his father. "I just want to have some confidence. I want to know that I can maybe be a good football player."

Then Moore made a promise: "If you come back, you'll have the greatest friendships that you will ever have in your life. You'll develop confidence in yourself as a football player and you'll have fun." Walking over to the marker board in the bedroom, he wrote "Fun."

Lutkus tried to rein him in. "So is it your testimony that you didn't see Coach Moore hit any other players?"

"I mean, just like stuff like in the chest; I mean just grabbing face masks and stuff like that, but every coach does that, I mean pretty much."

It was apparent that Kaczenski wanted to protect Joe. Lutkus persisted. "Okay. When you said he hit you in the chest, what do you mean by that?"

"Just with your shoulder pads on, just trying to give you a shove or something like that."

"I mean, did Clevenger tell you that he had been hit?"

"I never heard him mention it at any other specific time except in that locker room at the spring game."

"Okay, did Doughty ever tell you later that he had been punched up under the face mask?"

"I don't know." Kaczenski suddenly jumped to his feet. "This is bullshit!" he bellowed, glaring at Lutkus and Hoye. "I don't even know why I'm here!" He started to walk away from the table but was caught by the small microphone attached to his t-shirt. In a rage, he ripped the microphone off, threw it on the table and rushed out of the room.

"My God, I think he's walking out on this," I whispered to Joe.

As we all were walking out to the lobby Joe, who was several feet from Davie, said in a stage whisper, "Can you believe they're putting these kids through this?"

Davie shot back. "*They're* putting them through this! *You're* putting them through this!"

"Yeah, you really care about the kids," Joe growled. The two men began to move toward each other. I quickly took Joe's arm and guided him toward the exit. "You believe this guy?" Joe said loudly, as Davie and his lawyers disappeared around the corner.

Ten minutes later, Kaczenski returned, having calmed down, and resumed his testimony. He told Lutkus that after Coach Moore convinced him to stay at Notre Dame, things immediately got better. "It's been the best three years of my life. This is the most fun I've ever had playing this game, and I'm so thankful I stayed here. I get a queasy feeling when I think I could have left here." He became Notre Dame's starting center, playing in the Orange Bowl even though he weighed only 240 pounds. "I felt Coach Moore had looked past a lot of things to get me in the lineup."

As Kaczenski went on praising Joe, Davie abruptly stood up and left the room.

He owed his college and football career to Coach Moore, Kaczenski said. Coach Moore was right about the friend-ships he would form on the team. "I mean, they're my best friends and we're that way because of how hard things were for us, the roller coaster we had emotionally, so we just did everything together. There's just a special nucleus." He re-ally missed the coach, who had taught Kaczenski that there was "much more to football than just football. Football teaches you about life."

Most important was Kaczenski's memory of what Davie had said at the December players' meeting: "He said Coach Moore's sixty-something and he wants some continuity, you know, something like that, and he didn't know how long he'd be around coaching."

When I talked to Lutkus several days later about a sched-uling matter, he mentioned Kaczenski. "He was supposed to be our witness, but it turned out he was yours."

But Notre Dame refused to concede the battle over the players: they issued a subpoena for Chris Clevenger, an of-fensive tackle who had also been in the spring game. Clev-enger refused to talk to me when I phoned him. Joe said he thought that Clevenger would want to please the university. But I had no grounds to quash the subpoena: deposing Cle-venger wouldn't violate Judge Sharp's two student-player rule because Clevenger had graduated and wasn't a player any longer.

At the deposition, Lutkus asked Clevenger to describe the spring 1995 game. Clevenger, looking like a young businessman with his dark suit and tie, replied that the offense played miserably throughout the first half. Just before half time, they ran play 19X—an outside zone play to the split end side, which Clevenger was assigned to cover. He tried but failed to reach his assignment, the defensive end. Coach Moore was close enough to see the missed block, and when the players came off the field, he screamed at him.

While Clevenger was sitting on the bench on the sideline, the coach got down on one knee in front of him and ranted on about his poor performance. To emphasize the point, he reached under Clevenger's helmet chin guard, and struck him four times in rapid succession under the chin with his fist.

A few minutes later when the players were coming down the tunnel to the locker room, Coach Moore's graduate assistant ushered the five offensive players into a small room and stood guard outside the door. The coach came in and stood in front of the five players, who were sitting on a bench in the same sequence as their positions on a line of scrimmage. "Take your fucking helmets off!" he screamed. In a rage, towering above them, he ripped apart their performance.

Working himself into a frenzy, he went down the line, randomly smashing his closed fist into the boys' cheeks, mouths and chins. Some were hit more than once. They sat in stunned silence as the rampage continued. When Coach Moore reached Clevenger, he paused, glared at him, and gave him a light rabbit punch on the forehead. Then the anger suddenly seemed to drain from him. He shook his head and growled, "Just get the fuck out of here."

Clevenger and the four others, furious and incredulous, went into the locker room. When Clevenger glanced into a small mirror there, he was astounded to see that his mouth and chin were covered with blood. He realized that the coach hadn't hit him hard in the face in the locker room only because he was already bleeding profusely from the punches that he had received on the sidelines.

When it was my turn to question him, Clevenger testified that he and Davie had had at least two private meetings about the Moore lawsuit, the most recent several days after Kaczenski's deposition. He had also met twice with the Notre Dame lawyers, once with Wadsworth present.

I asked him about the disciplinary charges brought against him the previous year by two female students who said he used a racial epithet to one of them. Clevenger said that Father William Beauchamp, whom Clevenger considered a friend, helped him to prepare his defense. He denied the allegations and was completely exonerated. But he testified that at the December players meeting, he heard Davie say, "Coach Moore's old, and I'm looking for a long-term commitment."

After the deposition, Joe, very upset about Clevenger's recitation of the locker room incident, insisted that Clevenger had deliberately exaggerated what had happened. "He was always a semi-coward, although I encouraged him to be more aggressive."

"He was pretty aggressive today," I murmured.

I began to worry that I was putting too much time and energy into this case. In addition to the many depositions, motions and investigation, Mimi and I talked for hours about every nuance of the lawsuit. We wondered whether the Notre Dame people were really as confident as they acted. Did they know something we didn't know? Could we trust the judge? Could we win before a jury?

No matter how confident a lawyer feels about a case at the outset, the ups and downs of pretrial discovery can shake even the most secure advocate. The possibility of losing a case didn't generally bother me. I had long ago accepted the truism that any lawyer who tries cases will lose cases. If a lawyer is afraid to lose, he or she can't be a trial lawyer. But in this case, I had developed a relationship with Joe beyond attorney and client. On the weekends, we talked about things like the personalities in the case, and Notre Dame's performance during a Saturday game. I didn't want to let Joe down; I was worried about what a loss would do to him. His identity was so involved with his sterling reputation as a coach, that I was afraid if that reputation were besmirched, it could destroy him.

I was also aware that by the fall, only eleven months after we started the case, Ross & Hardies had generated over a quarter of a million dollars in expenses and legal fees. A defeat would mean that the firm would incur a significant financial loss and of course that would affect me financially too. I was afraid I was neglecting my corporate clients and this case was swallowing me up. That fall I read *A Civil Action*—about a lawyer whose career was destroyed because of his obsession with a water pollution case. I decided that a good settlement, as soon as possible, would be best for the Moores and for Ross & Hardies. Settlement had to be the overriding objective.

Judge Sharp required parties to participate in settlement mediation conferences before a federal magistrate. He assigned our case to Magistrate Judge Andrew Rodovich in Hammond, Indiana. Shortly before the conference, we received a letter from Lutkus threatening to file a motion for Rule 11 sanctions unless we dropped our retaliation claim: he found no deposition testimony to support our claim that Notre Dame had retaliated against our threat to file a lawsuit by withdrawing its commitment to pay Joe's salary for a year and a half.

Rule 11 prohibits attorneys from pursuing a factually baseless claim and authorizes the court to issue severe sanctions against a lawyer who does that. I thought this threat was a tactic to intimidate us before the mediation conference, and force us to settle for a low figure. I realized that we couldn't substantiate the retaliation claim, but I felt that if we withdrew it, we would look weak.

I wrote to Lutkus outlining the basis for the retaliation claim: that during the settlement discussions in December, Carol Kaesebier had told us that Father William Beauchamp had decided that Notre Dame would continue Joe's salary for a year and a half, and that the decision was made before settlement talks began. But after settlement discussions broke down, in our final conversation she told us that Notre Dame would pay Joe for only six months—not for the year and a half. I wrote Lutkus that this revocation was "a blatant act of retaliation against Mr. Moore for having the temerity to raise an age discrimination claim."

In fact, I didn't want to put the lawyers in the middle of the retaliation claim. I was bluffing, hoping we could find convincing evidence to support the allegations.

Bill Wortel and I arrived in Hammond early and stopped for a second breakfast at a doughnut shop. While we were eating our bagels, I said, "Bill, don't let me weaken when we get into that conference."

He looked puzzled. "Why would you?"

"Well, Notre Dame knows they've been beating us up pretty good. I'm afraid if they put just enough minimally acceptable money on the table, I might be tempted to take it. I don't want to sell Joe short. We need to hang tough." Bill agreed with me that a minimally acceptable figure would be $450,000—of which $250,000 would reimburse the firm, and $200,000 would go to Joe. In fact, I knew I would be tempted to recommend that amount to Joe, even though I believed the case was worth more.

We arrived at the magistrate judge's outer office to be told by his secretary that the judge intended to meet with each side separately; the Notre Dame lawyers were already with him. After half an hour, Kaesebier, Lutkus and LaDue emerged, smiling and laughing, from the inner office. I introduced Bill Wortel to Carol Kaesebier; she greeted him warmly but was noticeably cool to me.

Bill and I entered a large old-fashioned office. Leather chairs faced an ornate wooden desk, on which Bill noticed a brief that appeared to have been submitted by Notre Dame. It was inappropriate, perhaps even unethical, for one party to submit a brief to a judge without advising the other party. And it was obvious that Magistrate Rodovich, a trim man in his early forties, had already formed an opinion. "This is a difficult case for you. I'm aware of the abuse issue; that your client hit players. That kind of evidence will not play well to an Indiana jury . . ."

I interrupted. "It might be useful, Your Honor, if I put that in context and give you our perspective on the case—a case we believe is very strong." I outlined the facts, but Judge Rodovich seemed unmoved.

"I agree you have enough evidence of age discrimination to get to a jury. I told the other side that they will not get the case thrown out on summary judgment by Judge Sharp. But when you get to the jury, I believe you will lose, between the abuse and the evidence that your client was planning to retire in a few years anyway. He'll get no sympathy from a jury. The most I could recommend to settle this case is one hundred and thirty thousand. That's not an offer from Notre Dame; it's my own bottom line recommendation."

I hadn't noticed the brief on his desk so I couldn't understand how he had decided so quickly on the merits of the case, after only a short oral briefing by Notre Dame. "With all due deference, Your Honor," I said, "we feel confident we will prevail. And our client intends to continue working for a long time. In fact, there are a number of college and football coaches who are well into their seventies. We could get up to ten years in front pay."

Judge Rodovich shook his head. "I closely follow jury verdicts in Indiana. There's no way you will get that much money, assuming you win. Between what an Indiana jury would give you for back pay and what Judge Sharp would give you for front pay, I can't recommend more than one hundred and thirty thousand to settle this case."

"Does that take into account our attorney's fees which, as you know, are also awarded to the prevailing party? We have approximately two hundred and fifty thousand of fees and expenses into this case so far."

"A hundred and thirty thousand is as high as I could in good faith recommend. You won't get more than that if you proceed with the case and I believe you will lose. Why don't you call your client and discuss this with him?"

My heart sank. After putting in so much time and effort in the case, I couldn't recommend to Joe that we take so little. By the time expenses were deducted, both Joe and Ross & Hardies would lose in every way. "I don't need to call Coach Moore," I said. "He feels strongly about this case as a matter of principle and he's willing to risk losing to vindicate himself. As for us, we're a big law firm—if we lose, we can take the hit. But I don't think that will happen. Thank you for your efforts."

Notre Dame had another brief session with the magistrate before leaving his office, no longer in a happy mood. Lutkus looked grim. "At least they understand now," I remarked to Bill, "that we're not going away for peanuts. Did he really think we were voluntarily going to take a bath on the case when we had a quarter of a million dollars in it?"

Shortly after this meeting, Notre Dame filed a motion for summary judgment on the retaliation claims. Judge Sharp promptly granted the motion, leaving only the age discrimination claims in the case.

The depositions continued in tandem with the football season. After losing five of its first seven games, Notre Dame began to win, generally by slim margins, mainly against a string of third-rate teams: Hawaii, Navy and West Virginia. As Notre Dame plodded from game to game, the litigants pounded away in deposition after deposition. Seven Notre Dame coaches were deposed during the week following Notre

Dame's squeaker win, 21 to 17, against Navy, a team that had not beaten Notre Dame since 1963. The coaches reported for their depositions, still talking about how Navy narrowly missed winning the game in the final seconds when a Navy receiver caught a forty-yard pass and was pushed out of bounds only one yard short of a touchdown.

The depositions alternated as if possession of the ball were changing from one team to the other. Notre Dame deposed a Disney executive who testified that he had often seen Joe abusing players on the sidelines, and I deposed Gerald Materne, who had tried to spy for Tulane. In their turn, Notre Dame deposed Davie's lawyer in the Tulane proceedings, who maintained that Davie was being unfairly accused.

As the parade of witnesses continued, I formed my own opinion about their truthfulness. But I was baffled by Jim Colletto, the offensive coordinator and line coach who had replaced Joe. He had a winning, teddy bear quality; it was impossible not to like him. His likeability may have been the reason for his repeatedly landing on his feet in his career, with an unusual number of job changes, even for a college coach. He had coached at UCLA, California Fullerton, Purdue, Brown, Xavier, University of the Pacific, Ohio State, Arizona State, and now Notre Dame. He himself said that his record as head coach at California Fullerton was not "what you call outstanding." His efforts at Purdue, immediately before coming to Notre Dame, resulted in an embarrassing 21-43-3 record and for his final year, he was only 3 and 8. By the end of his tenure at Purdue, Colletto was so exhausted that he considered quitting football. But he was able to use his considerable network of contacts to secure the plum job at Notre Dame.

Like most coaches, Colletto had his own training philosophy. He believed that offensive line positions are probably the most physical positions in football. No one gives
the offensive player an inch; the defensive player on the other
side of the field is intent on knocking his offensive
counterpart's head off and the offensive linemen must eliminate him through a variety of extremely aggressive techniques.
A successful player learns that, even though he may have
been kicked in the wrong place, poked in the eye or cut on
the shin, when the referee signals that the ball is ready for
play, he must be ready for that play within twenty-five seconds. No one cares whether a player's leg or eye is sore; if he
is not actually incapacitated, he must play despite his pain.
So of course he must be tough, and teaching these offensive
line players requires a certain type of coach. In all of Colletto's
coaching years, every offensive line coach he had ever encountered was rough and tough, and he believed that successful offensive linemen reflect the personalities of their
coaches. It seemed that successful coaches had to shout and
go to whatever lengths they thought necessary to motivate
players to smash their opponents on the field.

But when I asked Colletto whether he had ever abused a
player physically or psychologically, he flatly denied doing
that. He said that he had never struck Ryan Harmon or used
foul language against him. Indeed, Colletto swore that in his
entire career no one could ever say that he was an abusive
coach.

Toward the end of the deposition, I asked Colletto
whether he was aware that Bob Davie, Michael Wadsworth
and Father Beauchamp had testified that they had no knowledge of the Harmon lawsuit when they hired him. I was sur-

prised that the lawyers hadn't forestalled his refusal to confirm their story.

He said that when he was interviewed for the job in South
Bend, "the Harmon lawsuit came up the next morning in a
meeting with Davie, Wadsworth and Kelly" and he "knew
that Mike and Bob and George were aware of that because
they did look into that. . . . Whether they had a conversation
with [Purdue athletic director] Morgan Burke or the university attorneys about that, I'm not sure. But they do—from
what I can gather, and I'm just making an assumption here—
they do a fairly decent background check on coaches they
bring to Notre Dame."

Colletto, who clearly did not want to leave the impression that he had suppressed information to get the job, said
he told Wadsworth, Kelly and Davie that the case was
dropped. "Two different attorneys dealt with it. There was
an investigation of Ryan Harmon himself that uncovered
use of drugs and alcohol and all kinds of things that he was
doing that was not very productive for him as an individual
. . . no player could corroborate all the things he said that I
did to him, and that's a whole lot of players." So Colletto
said he told his three prospective bosses that "basically, the
suit was dropped, and we went on from there."

This testimony clearly changed the picture. Whether
Colletto engaged in misconduct was now less important than
the fact that the university had tried to hide its knowledge of
Harmon's allegations of abuse when Colletto was hired. It
was obvious that whatever concerns Notre Dame may have
had about Joe and his relationship with players, they must
have had similar concerns about Colletto's conduct and they

had hired him anyway. I hoped this would be powerful evidence before a jury—that Notre Dame's abuse defense was simply a pretext to hide the real reason Davie fired Joe.

Notre Dame ended the 1997 season with six losses—the most defeats suffered by the team since the mid-1980s before Holtz and Moore took over. The only competitive team they beat in 1997 was Louisiana State, but in a bowl game after the season, Notre Dame lost to LSU, 27-9.

In the final polls, Notre Dame wasn't even ranked in the top twenty-five. Its rushing attack when Joe was coaching the year before, had ranked eighth. Now it ranked thirty-eighth. And Purdue, which had had a 3-8 season in 1996 under Colletto, won nine of its twelve games in 1997 with most of the same players, and ranked fifteenth in the nation.

Summing up his first season as head coach, Davie told reporters, "It's been like it's been this year."

As the case progressed through the winter and spring of 1998 toward the July trial date, Notre Dame began filing fourth quarter motions with the court. In one motion, Judge Sharp was asked to dismiss the remainder of the case—the age discrimination claims. The judge declined to do so, but expressed serious doubts about the legal validity of our case. The university also asked Judge Sharp to exclude all evidence concerning allegations of abuse by Colletto and of Davie's actions at Arizona and Tulane. The judge denied that motion too, but said he would reconsider it at trial.

As the trial date approached, we waited in vain for Notre Dame to reopen settlement discussions. I began to believe

that the lull in press coverage had removed any incentive
they might have had to settle the case. Joe said of course
they disliked bad press, but they probably felt that the worst
was over "after all the fuss when we filed the case. Now
most people don't even realize the case is still going on."
Obviously the only way to put settlement pressure on Notre
Dame was to get the case back in the news.

In late spring, I hired Mary Beth Berkoff to handle public relations for us, and she began working her connections
with television newsmagazines. ABC and NBC weren't interested, but a "60 Minutes" producer said that the suit
sounded interesting. Unfortunately, the program was about
to take its summer hiatus and wouldn't resume production
before the trial. That would be too late for national publicity to force Notre Dame into serious settlement discussions.

As time went on, I began to think that Notre Dame knew
what they were doing. Rather than settle for a significant
sum, they had probably decided to go to trial and risk a
four-line AP wire story buried in the back of the sports sections.

After weeks of disappointments, Mary Beth telephoned
to tell me to call Lester Munson, who wrote for *Sports
Illustrated*'s "Score Card," probably the most popular section of the magazine because it dealt with hard news, including sports scandals. Munson asked me whether there were
any older coaches in college football. I had an Internet list of
senior college coaches: "Absolutely. Joe Paterno of Penn State,
seventy-one, Iowa's Hayden Fry, sixty-nine, Bobby Bowden
of Florida State, sixty-eight, and LaVell Edwards of Brigham
Young, sixty-seven."

The article, headed "Will You Still Need Me?" after the
Beatles song, appeared in the *Sports Illustrated* issue for July
1st. It was sympathetic to Joe, ending with the comment:
"When this case is over, the Fighting Irish may wish they
hadn't fought this one out."

This article was a catalyst for a flood of press inquiries.
Mary Beth had sent out a press release naming me as the
contact for information, and a week before the trial, reporters began to call. J.R. Ross of the AP said he would cover the
trial if a death penalty execution in Indiana was postponed.
Roman Modrowski, just assigned to cover college football
for the *Chicago Sun-Times*, also expressed an interest. I told
him that this story deserved his attention, and to my surprise, he readily agreed: "Oh, we're definitely going to cover
this on an extensive basis. I'll be there at the trial every day
and we'll run a major preview piece."

As the calls came in, I worked hard to urge the reporters
on. But Notre Dame made no move to settle the case. The
press strategy was working, but a week before the trial, only
the *Sports Illustrated* article had run and Notre Dame did
not appear to be aware that the press might be circling, ready
to attack. A week before the trial, Michael Wadsworth told
the *South Bend Tribune*: "It hasn't been wearing on me."

The *Tribune* reserved a huge space on its front page, and
on Sunday, three days before the trial, Dave Haugh's story
about the case ran under a banner headline. That was the
good news. Haugh, using portions of the deposition transcripts that were in the public record, reviewed the testimony
in detail. But the bad news was that Haugh focused on Davie's
comments about Joe's behavior and the accusations of player

abuse. For the first time, the claims against Joe were on public display. I hoped that he wouldn't see the article.

Haugh questioned also whether we had attempted to extort a huge settlement from Notre Dame, whose director of public relations said, "They have made one offer [to settle] and essentially they wanted to make Joe Moore a millionaire. They have never budged from what we regard as an attempt to hold us hostage."

"I saw your article," I said to Haugh on the phone the next day.

"Well," he said, "you know I need to be balanced in reporting this."

The AP story that ran throughout the country on the first day of trial, also featured the abuse theme: "Court papers suggest Notre Dame will introduce a slough of incidents in which Moore is said to have punched, pushed and abused players."

LEFT: Notre Dame football coach Bob Davie arrives at the federal courthouse in Lafayette, Indiana.
(AP/Worldwide Photos)

BELOW: Fran and Joe Moore leave the courthouse after Judge Sharp's decision is handed down.
(AP/Worldwide Photos)

LEFT: Notre Dame counsel Gerald Lutkus, right, and Bob Davie. (AP/Worldwide Photos)

LOWER LEFT: Judge Allen Sharp, in his chambers.

BELOW: Mimi Moore, the associate lawyer working on the case with Rick Lieberman.

Rick Lieberman and Joe Moore arrive at court. (AP/Worldwide Photos)

ABOVE: Rev. William Beauchamp, left, and Notre Dame athletic director Mike Wadsworth smile during a news conference in 1966, where the two announced the hiring of Bob Davie as the school's football coach. (AP/Worldwide Photos)

LEFT: Lou Holtz watches his team warm up on November 16, 1996. Holtz resigned several days later. (AP/Worldwide Photos)

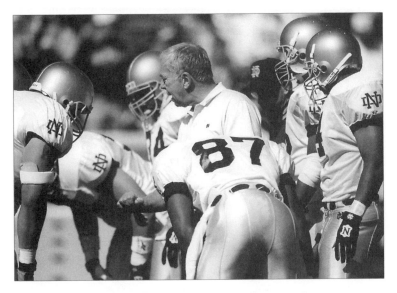

ABOVE: Joe Moore talking to Notre Dame linemen during a game.
BELOW: Joe on the sidelines with Lou Holtz. (Courtesy Joe Moore)

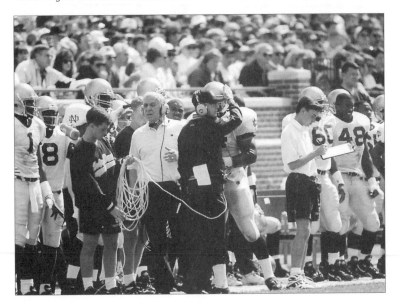

V

———

TRIAL: LAFAYETTE, INDIANA

As the Moores made the long drive from Pennsylvania to Indiana, they were well aware that what had started as Joe's case against Notre Dame would now also be Notre Dame's case against Joe. The lawsuit filed to vindicate him could end up destroying his most important professional asset: his reputation. A year and a half earlier, when they had come to Chicago to meet with us, they had not foreseen that there would actually be a real trial where Joe had as much to lose as to win.

During the drive, Fran jotted down questions to ask us when they reached Lafayette. "What about this, Fran?" Joe would sometimes say in his gruff voice, coming up with another idea, and Fran would occasionally say, "No, I already have a question like that." So it went, back and forth, the Fran-and-Joe partnership devising key questions to help win their case. "That's a good one," Joe said often, "write that down, Fran." When they ran out of questions for the lawyers, Joe had a question for Fran. "What are we gonna say to our family and friends if we lose this?" She didn't have an answer.

When they arrived at the Homewood Suites hotel on the outskirts of Lafayette, they found Mimi, Bill Wortel and me in the parking lot, unloading the document boxes that filled the entire interior of my van. Mimi said to them, "Guess who else is staying here? The entire Notre Dame trial team, their witnesses and technical people to operate their video equipment. I ran into Davie in the lobby, and he started talking to me, kidding around like I was his good friend. He asked where I went to school, and when I told him St. Mary's, he was shocked." She blushed.

Joe pulled me aside. "We have a list of questions we want to talk to you about, but first I want to ask you something."

"Sure, Joe. What?"

"What's your record?"

I looked at him, and for a minute I didn't get it. Then I began to laugh. The trial is starting tomorrow and now he asks me about my trial record, I thought. I love this guy.

Later that evening, as I walked down the hotel corridor to my room, a short portly man wearing a long dress shirt over bathing trunks and black dress shoes, passed me and nodded. He looked vaguely familiar. I turned as the figure retreated. "Good evening, Judge Sharp," I shouted down the hallway. My God, I thought, there must be dozens of hotels in this town, and everyone is staying here.

The United States District Court for the Northern District of Indiana, Lafayette Division, is located on the second floor of a nondescript 1930s post office building. It presents a considerable architectural contrast to the impressive state courthouse which dominates Lafayette's city square several blocks away. On the first morning of trial, Joe and I circled past the building several times searching for the courthouse, until we realized we were looking at it.

Lafayette is an agricultural, university, and white collar town which could provide an extremely varied jury pool. Joe and I walked toward the court building, where a couple of television people and a photographer were standing on the steps. I told them that Joe was eager to have his day in court. But my focus had shifted from courting the media to jury selection. I wanted a jury of working-class men who could relate to Joe.

Taking a tiny old elevator to the second floor, we walked into a large courtroom which probably still looked the way it had during the Depression. Mimi, Bill and Fran were already there; Mimi and Bill were busy organizing files and checking video equipment. David Haugh, sitting in the pew-like seats, introduced me to J.R. Ross of the Associated Press and Roman Modrowski of the *Chicago Sun-Times*. Three or four other reporters whom I didn't know were there, as well as several artists with sketch pads.

Bob Davie strolled into the courtroom, surrounded by his four lawyers—Gerald Lutkus, William Hoye, Carol Kaesebier and John LaDue—and a university public relations spokesman. Davie, looking tanned after a recent vacation, seemed relaxed, as if he were merely going to give a speech to the local Kiwanis Club.

I seated Joe on the left side of our counsel table near the empty jury box, so the jurors could easily see him. I sat in the middle of the table with Mimi on my right. Bill was in charge of the documents and exhibits piled against the wall several feet from our table. To our right, the Notre Dame contingent, including three video technicians, were sitting or standing around their table.

We wanted to present the jury with a David and Goliath contest, and Notre Dame had obliged us. Their team appeared all-powerful: a bevy of lawyers and support staff in dark blue suits, clustered around the glowing, charismatic Davie. I hoped that our team—Joe, weathered, salt-of-the-earth; Mimi, fresh, schoolgirlish, and Bill, young and eager—would present the jury with a favorable contrast. I wore a fifteen-year-old grey suit, neatly pressed, but nothing to compare with the elegant, expensive clothes at the other table. I believe that a jury's visual impression of the litigants, both lawyers and witnesses, is as important as the testimony. I hoped that their side would look strong and arrogant and our people, earnest and straightforward. I told them to just act naturally.

Judge Sharp entered the bench, wasting no time getting down to business. As the first order of business, he announced that he would allow no evidence of pre-Notre Dame misconduct by Davie or Moore. He made clear that he, not the lawyers, was going to control this trial. "This is an age discrimination case, and I'm going to keep it as an age discrimination case," he said, looking directly at me. "If you or they go out of bounds, I'll declare a mistrial." My heart sank. All the time and effort on Materne and Arizona was going to go for nothing. I considered asking the judge for his reasoning but thought better of it. Searching for something positive about the ruling, I whispered to Mimi, "Well, at least he's letting in the Colletto stuff."

Judge Sharp had an unusual procedure for opening statements. Before the jury was selected, the lawyers presented their opening statements to the entire jury pool; in this case, twenty-six Caucasian men and women sitting in the spectator seats in the courtroom.

I went first, turning away from the judge so that I could address the whole room. I wanted to make clear who Joe was: how, coming from a Pennsylvania working-class family, he had slowly worked his way up through the coaching ranks from high school to college football and finally to Notre Dame. I told them that the Notre Dame football program had fallen on hard times before Lou Holtz and Joe Moore arrived, described the extraordinary performance of the teams during the nine-year Holtz-Moore partnership, and went into how the program had fallen on hard times again when they left, as reflected by the dismal past season.

I told them that Joe had recruited Davie to come to Notre Dame, had acted as Davie's mentor, and that when Davie had achieved football's dream job, he had brutally fired Joe because he felt he couldn't count on a man Joe's age to last the full five years of Davie's contract.

I explained that it was only after Joe was fired that Notre Dame came up with hundreds of reasons why they had let him go—all phony, designed to hide age discrimination. One of those reasons was that Joe had been abusive to players. But that could not be a real reason for the firing because Davie hired Jim Colletto, a man who had a nationally known reputation for player abuse, as Joe's replacement.

As I started to talk about Colletto's background, Judge Sharp interrupted me to say that I was violating the exclusionary ruling.

I was amazed. While the exclusion of the Tulane and Arizona matters were severely disappointing, those were not critical to our case. Colletto, however, was absolutely essential because his hiring established that Davie did not really care about player treatment. I paused only for a moment, to cover the destructive impact of the ruling, and confidently finished my statement.

Back at the table, I muttered to Mimi, "Where the hell did that come from?"

When it was Lutkus's turn, he told the jury pool that Davie's decision not to renew Moore's contract had absolutely nothing to do with age. During the two-year period that he worked with Moore, Davie had had a unique opportunity to observe literally hundreds of reasons for firing him. The principal reason was player abuse, which Lutkus described to the jury. Another reason was continuity: Davie's legitimate desire to have a stable coaching staff. It was Moore's own expressed intention to quit coaching in a year or two, that was simply echoed by Davie in his meeting with Moore on December 2nd. Davie never said that he needed younger coaches or that Moore was too old.

I was more pleased with Lutkus's opening statement than with my own. All Notre Dame had to prove was that age was not a determining factor in Davie's decision, but Lutkus had flatly denied that age played any role in the decision at all, setting up a contest on the believability of the dueling witnesses. He implicitly attacked the credibility of the players, ignoring their testimony about Davie's age references, which we would introduce during the trial. Apparently, his strategy would be to focus on abuse, and expect the jury to lose sight of the evidence of age discrimination. I didn't intend to let that happen.

Jury selection can take days or weeks, but Judge Sharp believed that the eight jurors required for a civil case could be chosen in a couple of hours. He, not the lawyers, questioned the twenty-eight potential jurors. After twenty minutes he ascertained, among other things, that most of the jurors had seen Davie on television coaching Notre Dame games and had read about the Moore case in the newspapers. None of them had ever filed a discrimination claim. As the judge asked questions, the jurors responded by raising their hands. Mimi and I frantically tried to follow which jurors were responding to particular questions, and make detailed notes of their responses. Since the jurors had not yet been identified by name or number, we had to identify them in our notes by physical description.

Each side could eliminate up to three jurors without stating a reason. However, if good cause—clear bias—existed, any number of jurors could be struck "for cause." We wanted working-class male jurors, but the pool was predominantly made up of white-collar women. Judge Sharp called eight individuals to the jury box and permitted the lawyers to use their challenges on any of them. As each potential juror was challenged and excused, another would take his place. We eliminated, among others, two men who were high school football and wrestling coaches, fearing they would dominate the jury with their own opinions of proper coaching conduct. It was simply too risky to leave them on. We also excluded a woman who worked in personnel. Lutkus excluded a blue-collar union worker and an unemployed young man. Within an hour the jury was selected: five women and three men. Only two were over forty and all were employed. Four had college degrees, three from Purdue. One didn't have a high school diploma. Their jobs covered a broad spectrum: truck driver, medical technology researcher, bookkeeper, businessman/farmer, mapmaker, management consultant, secretary and legal secretary.

Mimi and I would have liked more male jurors, given Notre Dame's focus on physical abuse. Joe was afraid of the businessman/farmer. "That kind of self-reliant guy doesn't believe in age discrimination laws," he whispered. Mimi was worried about the smiling young male mapmaker who seemed excited about being on the jury. She thought he might be too eager. We all liked the middle-aged, slightly overweight truck driver with no high school diploma. As we left the courtroom for the morning recess, a reporter whispered to me, "You can't be too happy with so many women on the jury." He was right.

High tech electronic and video equipment, installed by the two parties, filled the old courtroom: computers, monitors, and cables throughout the well of the courtroom, and a large movie screen directly in front of the jury box. This was my first experience with this kind of equipment and I was skeptical about it. However, as soon as Mimi called our first witness, Stanford's Earl Mosley , I began to change my mind. Because Mosley was out of subpoena range, Judge Sharp permitted portions of his video-taped deposition to be shown. When Mosley appeared, bigger than life, on the screen, the jury seemed mesmerized as he testified forcefully about

Davie's conversation with him about Joe's age and retirement plans. I whispered excitedly to Mimi, "This is better than a live witness!"

Notre Dame showed Mosley's testimony about the racial incident at Boston College and Holtz's assault on him. They evidently wanted to demonstrate that Mosley was biased against Notre Dame—I wondered whether it was wise to risk bringing Lou Holtz's reputation into question.

Joe, wearing a blue blazer and a funereal expression, testified next. It was critical, I believed, that the jury know Joe so they would empathize with him. For several hours, I elicited an oral self-portrait. Speaking softly at first, and gradually gaining confidence, Joe described his job as a Notre Dame coach who had responsibility for all aspects of the players' lives—academic, social, and emotional, not just for their athletic performance.

When I asked him to put aside modesty and talk about his accomplishments at Notre Dame, Joe said that his "number one accomplishment" was that every one of his offensive line players had graduated from the university. He was proud, too, that virtually every kid on his line played at least one year for the National Football League; that a number of his players made All-American (designated by AP and UPI as the top college football players in the country); and that one player was selected as an Academic All-American. His greatest honor was his induction into Notre Dame's Monogram Club.

I used the large screen to show a letter on Notre Dame stationery from Father Beauchamp to Joe, written only nine months before his firing, expressing his deep gratitude for Joe's personal contribution to Notre Dame's successful football program, and saying—we underscored this statement in bright yellow—that he appreciated "the outstanding manner in which you represent the University and its mission." Enclosed with the letter was a bonus check for Joe's participation in the Orange Bowl.

After that I screened the March 22, 1995, reprimand letter Joe received from Lou Holtz because of the slapping incident—to let the jury know about our Achilles heel before Notre Dame could tell them about it. I tried to ameliorate Holtz's warning that there was "talk going around that you physically abused the offensive linemen at halftime of the spring game" which "wouldn't be tolerated by me or Notre Dame" with the complimentary part of the letter: "Your players have had great respect for you and loved you. You have been a positive coach who loved your players and showed them tremendous respect, and they responded by performing well above their physical skills." Joe testified that he had never received an oral or written reprimand before or after this, and Davie did not, at any time, mention to him the reprimand or the circumstances that prompted it.

Joe talked about how he had recruited Davie, and that he "thought we were friends." He described the details of the December firing and the final "fuck you" conversation with Davie.

Then Lutkus took over, moving immediately to the spring 1995 game. "Do you remember after Clevenger came off the field, you knelt down on one knee in front of him and you punched him up under the chin; do you remember that?"

"I thought I smacked him across the face."

"In full view of anyone who was watching at Notre Dame stadium; is that right?"

"If they were watching."

"In the locker room, you stood over Doughty first and you punched him in the face twice; isn't that right?"

"No."

"What did you do?"

"I smacked him."

"With your open hand?"

"Yes."

"Then you moved on to the next player in line?"

"Yes."

"Did you smack that player too?"

"Yes."

"How many times?"

"I think I only smacked them all once."

Lutkus was doing an excellent job—building the testimony to a crescendo. "In your testimony earlier, you said that this group of offensive linemen, this younger group of offensive linemen, had a lot of potential. Was this a way of getting their potential out, by going down and smacking them all on the face?"

Joe turned to the jury, maintaining his calm. "I made a drastic mistake that day."

"Did you apologize to Mike Doughty?" Lutkus asked.

"I told all of the kids that I made a mistake."

"Did you apologize to the parents of Akers, Clevenger or Leahy?"

Here Judge Sharp interrupted, with a wry smile. "You're getting close to a major point, Counsel?"

Lutkus had gone too far, but went one step farther. "You were aware that striking people like that is an illegal act, weren't you?"

Joe remained calm. "I told you I knew I had done something drastically wrong. I was very disappointed in myself."

Lutkus asked Joe if he had punched Clevenger and Doughty at the 1994 Florida game. "You punched Mike Doughty in the forehead, didn't you, at halftime?"

"You mean haul off and punch him?" Joe paused. "No."

"Did you smack him in the forehead?"

"I probably went over and I'd go like this to him." Joe demonstrated a tap on the forehead with the palm of his hand. "I probably hit 'em all just the way I demonstrated. 'Let's get going.' Like that."

Lutkus then directed Joe's attention to the 1996 Notre Dame–Navy game in Ireland. Joe had, had he not, forced players from their hotel rooms in the middle of the night, to a gravel parking lot and ordered them to do "up-downs"—repeatedly running in place, dropping to push-up position and jumping up.

The judge called a recess. As Joe and I walked alone down the long corridor outside the courtroom, I told him he was doing a great job. "But when he finishes, I'm going to ask you to tell the whole Ireland story."

"But, Rick, I didn't see it. I just heard about it."

"I don't care whether you saw it or not—just tell the story. Trust me on this, Joe."

Consequently on redirect, I asked Joe about what had happened in Ireland.

"Well, I was assigned bed-check, and that evening I called down to the front desk and told them that my name was Joe Moore, one of the Notre Dame coaches, and that if there were any problems with the football team, to let me know so I could talk to them. I guess it was around a quarter to eleven—the kids had to be in their rooms by eleven. I went upstairs and started shooing them into their rooms. About twenty minutes after eleven the front desk called and said that there was some commotion up there. There were airplane pilots on the same floor that had to fly out in the morning and they were complaining."

He said that on three separate occasions the front desk phoned him about the noise; each time he went up to find the kids out of control, jumping up and down and cheering and hollering. "Eventually I found out that the disturbance was that two of the . . ." he hesitated, embarrassed. "Basically they were having oral sex."

Outraged, Lutkus jumped to his feet. "Objection, Your Honor!"

Joe tried to go on. "Two of the cheerleaders were—"

Lutkus cried, "This is clearly based on hearsay!"

"You opened this door," the judge said to him. "Now sit down! Your objection is overruled."

Joe picked up his narrative once more. "And the players later informed me that a lot of the commotion was over two of the cheerleaders that were having oral sex. It was a U-shaped hotel and they could see across." He shook his head. "I was really, you know, disturbed to hear that people that have that kind of important job, flying an airplane, couldn't get to sleep. They said they had early flights. That's what the woman downstairs told me." Joe said he told the players they could explain their behavior to Coach Holtz or they could do up-downs until they were tired enough to go to bed. It was their choice, and they chose the up-downs.

Had anyone ever told him that he had acted improperly that evening? "To the contrary," he replied. "In fact, one coach said that he was glad to see somebody that cared enough to do something about the disturbance, that somebody would stand up and tell the kids they were doing wrong. Nobody ever mentioned a thing to me until I was deposed."

"Did anybody ever tell you that one of the reasons that Mr. Davie fired you was for taking this action that evening in Ireland?"

"Nobody ever mentioned anything to me."

At the end of the day, we avoided the crowded elevator, and walked down. A reporter was lying in wait at the foot of the stairs. "Rick, male and female or same sex?" he asked breathlessly.

I knew the answer—it was male and female. But I told him I really didn't know.

Newspapers across the country carried the AP story on the first day of the trial. Ironically, Lou Holtz, who had nothing to do with the case, had been thrust into the spotlight by Notre Dame's presentation of his assault on Mosley. The press asked Holtz for a statement, but he didn't respond.

While I was getting dressed for the second trial day, I received call after call from reporters. A producer from "Good Morning America" wanted to do a satellite feed interview from Lafayette; a Los Angeles sports radio show asked for an immediate interview. Overnight, the case had attracted national attention—too late, it seemed to me, for Notre Dame to settle, even if they wanted to. I politely declined the interview requests, and left for court.

Mimi's first witness was Fran, who described, in her matter-of-fact, no-nonsense way, Joe's firing at their apartment on December 2nd. As she spoke, I watched the impassive women on the jury, and wondered how they could doubt her story. But of course they might think she would lie to protect her husband.

We showed the video testimony of Mike Rosenthal, Rick Kaczenski and Chris Clevenger, their images on the screen bigger than life. Rosenthal, photogenic and respectful, looked like the quintessential Notre Dame football player. The courtroom was rapt as he testified that Davie mentioned Joe's age when he explained the firing to the players, and as he described his grief at the loss of the coach who was the most important influence in his life.

We knew that the Clevenger testimony would give Lutkus the opportunity, in cross examination, to elicit Clevenger's damaging description of Joe's pugnacious behavior toward him at the 1994 Florida game. But we felt we had to call him, because Clevenger had also testified that Davie told the players that Moore was old—this was powerful ammunition for our side, and anyway, we knew that Notre Dame would use Clevenger's harmful testimony no matter what we did.

Clevenger's testimony had other helpful aspects. To counter Davie's claim that Joe was fired, in part, for drinking with players, there was Clevenger's testimony that another Notre Dame coach had smoked and drunk with a group of players at a party in the past season. And Clevenger provided a detailed description of the players hooting and hollering as they leered through the window of the Dublin hotel at the two lusty cheerleaders. Finally, Clevenger talked about his respect for Joe: "I learned a great deal about football and about life from him." Coach Moore helped him more than anyone else, Clevenger said, and when he was recruiting high school athletes for Notre Dame, he told them that Moore was "a great coach." Several days after the firing, Clevenger went with a group of offensive linemen to the coach's apartment, where Clevenger gave Joe an expensive putter that he had bought for him the day before. "I thought it was a good idea to show him that he had done a lot for me and I appreciated it."

Justin Hall, the former graduate assistant coach, flew in from Nevada to testify on Joe's behalf. On the stand, he explained how two days after the termination, Davie told him that he believed Joe was only going to coach another year or two, that he needed someone who would be there longer than that, and that he ended by saying, "Christ, let's face it, he's sixty-four years old." Hall told the jury, "That statement kind of stuck with me the whole time because it didn't really make sense, because I believed Joe would coach forever."

I had tried to build a case of age discrimination, like a wall, brick by brick. Now the wall was half-completed. During the first day of testimony and half of the second, we had presented supportive witnesses and evidence to show the jury that we had a strong case. But completing the wall would be much more difficult: I would have to call Father William Beauchamp, Michael Wadsworth and Bob Davie as hostile witnesses.

It is often considered unnecessarily risky to a case to call adverse witnesses. It's like a general calling on enemy soldiers to help him; they could easily turn and shoot him. But I thought it was worth the risk to try and forestall Lutkus's showing these three men in the most favorable light. I hoped to damage their credibility before Lutkus could build them up.

I had to proceed cautiously with Father Beauchamp, of course; I certainly did not want to be seen making an attack on a priest. All I wanted from him was testimony that Davie told him that he fired Joe principally because Joe was a poor recruiter of players. That would be important because Davie, at his deposition, while giving many other reasons for the firing, had specifically said that he didn't know anything about Joe's recruiting skills.

Father Beauchamp was a trim middle-aged man with salt-and-pepper hair. He was wearing his collar, and identified himself as a priest of the Congregation of Holy Cross, and secondly as the Executive Vice President of the University of Notre Dame, holding degrees in Divinity, Law, and Business Administration.

I asked him whether he was responsible, among other things, for the Notre Dame athletic programs.

"I have numerous responsibilities," he replied.

I repeated the question. William Hoye, the Notre Dame in-house lawyer, objected. Eventually, Father Beauchamp answered. "One of my areas of responsibility is overall over-sight for the athletic program, yes."

"Am I correct that Mr. Davie told you at the time of his interview process that the reason he was not going to keep Coach Moore was that he felt Coach Moore was not an adequate recruiter of players?"

"That was one of the issues that was discussed regarding Coach Moore. One of the concerns expressed was about recruiting, was one of the areas. That was not the only one, though."

"With respect to recruiting, am I correct that Mr. Davie said that Moore was not involved in recruiting or had had very little involvement in recruiting, in Mr. Davie's view?"

"I don't recall Bob Davie's exact words, except that it was indicated that he was not involved in the same manner as the rest of the assistant coaches."

I didn't intend to let him get away with this vague answer. "You remember we took your deposition under oath some months ago. Page twenty-five, line eleven, a question from me: 'Okay. As best you recall, what did Davie say to you, and what did you say to Davie regarding the matter of Moore at this time?' Answer—and this is you speaking, Father—'My best recollection is that there was a concern expressed by Bob Davie about Joe Moore not being an adequate recruiter and not being involved in recruiting or having very little involvement in recruiting.' Does that refresh your recollection?"

"That would be an accurate statement."

But when I asked Father Beauchamp to confirm that poor recruiting and extended lunch hours were the only reasons Davie expressed for dismissing Moore, he again equivocated. "Those are the two that specifically stand out in my mind, but I would not say that that's the only reasons, but those two specifically stand out in my mind, yes."

"When I took your deposition a few months ago, those were the only two things that you could recall that Mr. Davie mentioned?"

"At that particular meeting when we met with Bob Davie, yes." But he added: "That is not the only discussion we had regarding Joe Moore."

"Those are the only two concerns you have a recollection of him expressing?"

"That's right," he agreed, reluctantly.

"You've got no notes or other documents that would provide any other reason that Davie expressed to you as to why he would not keep Coach Moore?"

"At that specific meeting?" he asked.

"At the meetings around Mr. Davie being interviewed and expressing his view as to why he would not keep Coach Moore."

"That would be correct." But he added another caveat: with respect to "overall conversations that were not necessarily meetings where there was some discussion of Joe Moore, that would not be accurate."

I knew that unless I made it crystal clear, the jury would miss the point. "Let me ask you this: is it true that during the entire period of Coach Moore's tenure at Notre Dame, nine years, up to and including the time of his termination, that no one, including Mr. Davie over here, ever brought to your attention any criticism of Joe Moore regarding his interaction with players?"

He had no intention of conceding this. "That is not correct," he said. "I don't know what you mean by 'interaction with players.' If you're talking about in terms of coaching the players and his overall coaching with the players, there was some concern expressed by Bob Davie's predecessor."

"I'm talking about his dealings with the student athletes."

"As I said, I don't know what you mean by 'dealings.' As a coach, there were some concerns expressed. Coaching involves dealings."

I read slowly from Father Beauchamp's deposition: "'There were some instances that came to my attention re-garding Joe Moore's performance after—'" I paused for a moment for emphasis "'—after he was terminated regarding what I would consider problems in his dealings with student athletes, but I was not aware of those, was not made aware of those prior to that time.' Does that refresh your recollection?"

He gave up. "As I said, if you're talking about specific instances regarding his treatment of student athletes, that would be correct."

Fran Moore, watching Beauchamp from the rear of the courtroom, was shocked and bitterly disappointed at his testimony.

Michael Wadsworth was the next witness. He took the stand exuding confidence. Referring to his deposition testimony, I asked, "And the reason Mr. Davie stated he would replace Coach Moore was because he believed that Mr. Moore was not fully committed to the recruiting of players; isn't that correct?"

"No, it's not." Davie, he said, "was not talking about the reasons for not keeping individuals." In fact, he didn't recall that Davie "went through specifics with respect to any of the positions that he wanted to change, the reason why."

"Maybe," I said, "we can try to refresh your recollection, sir." I read from his deposition the question about whether Davie had given Wadsworth reasons for replacing the offensive people, and Wadsworth's answer: "'A large part of it in relation to Coach Moore was that he had to have somebody who was going to be able to be one hundred percent into recruiting when required.'" I read the next question: "'Any other reasons that he set forth?'" to which Wadsworth's answer was "'No.'" Did that, I asked him, refresh his recollection that Davie had told him he was firing Moore because of recruiting?

"It refreshes my recollection, but . . ."

"Good." I interrupted, trying to cut him off.

But he went on. "I would take issue with the fact that those questions and answers reflect necessarily that Coach Davie had said that Coach Moore did not do certain things as a coach. All I was saying in my original answer to you, and what I would still say with the benefit of the assistance you've given me on the deposition, is that Coach Davie, my recollection still is, in our meeting—the lengthy meeting he had with the committee—was talking in terms of what was going to be very important to him in terms of the staff he would assemble. And putting together the staff he would assemble, one of the things that was very important was a staff that gives full commitment to recruiting."

"All right. Maybe you and I are having problems with the English language, but did you understand when you testified under oath about using the word 'reasons'—that was the reason expressed by Mr. Davie? Or were you confused somehow by those questions and answers?" He continued to equivocate, but I felt that I had made my point.

Trying to show that Notre Dame immediately understood that Joe's firing involved an age discrimination issue, I asked, "Now, in the December, 1996, period, after Coach Moore was told that he was terminated by Mr. Davie—and this is before the lawyers got involved, before any lawyers—am I correct that it came to your attention that Mr. Moore was raising complaints that he had been wronged by virtue of age discrimination?"

"It had come to my attention after, I would say some days after they had the meeting, that is, Coach Davie and Coach Moore had their meeting. I would say it was a matter of days after that that I became aware of some unhappiness on Coach Moore's part."

"I take it the answer to my question is 'yes'?"

"Yes," he conceded reluctantly.

"At the time these complaints were raised, you knew that Mr. Moore was sixty-four, sixty-five years old?"

"That's correct. I knew from the letter that I reviewed earlier approximately what his age was."

"It is against the policy of Notre Dame, is it not, to discriminate against employees on the basis of their age?"

"Absolutely."

"And you knew you could not take age into account in assessing whether to retain or not retain an assistant coach at Notre Dame; isn't that correct?"

"That's correct."

I paused for effect. "So after learning a few days later, that Coach Moore—nine years with the program, sixty-four, sixty-five years old—it comes to your attention that this man is complaining, saying, 'Something has happened to me; I've been thrown out because of my age,'—did you interview Coach Moore just to ask him, 'What's going on, Joe?'"

Wadsworth straightened in his chair and answered firmly, "I did not."

Incredulously, I asked, "Did you make any efforts to reach out to Coach Moore in terms of finding out what his problem was?"

"I suspected what some of the problem was."

"No. I said, 'Did you make any efforts to reach out to him, call him, contact him, any efforts at all?'"

"I didn't feel at that point—"

"No, I'm not asking how you felt, I'm asking did you or didn't you?"

Judge Sharp intervened. "Wait a minute, Counsel. One question at a time. Slow down and cool it."

Emphasizing each word, I asked, "Did you make any efforts—any efforts—to reach out to this man who had given nine years of his life to the university, who had been in the forefront of keeping Notre Dame's football program in the limelight and who you knew had been fired by this new young coach—he's complaining about age discrimination—did you make any efforts to contact him to find out what was wrong? Yes or no?"

"I did not because I didn't have any reason to."

"No reason?" I murmured, and turned the examination over to William Hoye, who elicited testimony that Wadsworth, far from showing a lack of concern, immediately turned the matter over to the university's general counsel's office.

I wasn't about to let this go. On redirect, I asked, "Just so we're clear, after you heard that Moore was complaining of age discrimination, you figured rather than reach out to him, this long-term employee, you would just let him go ahead and sue you; is that correct?"

"It wasn't a question of let him go ahead and sue me. It was a question of if he wants to pursue it as a litigious role, then we'll have our lawyers involved with it."

"So he would either sue you or he wouldn't get any satisfaction at all because you weren't going to do a thing about it; isn't that correct?"

"Excuse me," he said with some asperity. "We thought we were treating Coach Moore extremely fairly because we were giving him protection beyond the contract that he was entitled to. We thought that was pretty fair treatment. We thought every other coach was getting fair treatment. No other coach came up to us and said, 'You're not treating us fairly.' We thought that was pretty fair and reasonable."

I looked at the jury before I turned back to Wadsworth. "Your testimony is that you treated Coach Moore fairly?"

"That was certainly our intent," Wadsworth said.

I thought to myself that if the jury didn't recognize Notre Dame's arrogance at that point, they would never recognize it.

By noon of the second trial day, we had gone through nine witnesses; the case was moving much faster than we had anticipated. Davie was next: during lunch at a small cafe near the courthouse, while reporters and photographers crowded around Joe and Justin Hall, I sat apart, cramming for Davie's examination. I had been looking forward to taking him on since his deposition a year earlier. I had repeatedly told Mimi and Bill Wortel that it was essential to mess him up on the stand, and consequently I had spent days selecting portions of his videotaped deposition; each snippet was transferred to a computer, and marked by bar codes. But I was nervous about the technology; if there was a snafu, it would ruin the examination. It was also possible that Judge Sharp would not permit me to do what I intended.

Davie took the stand that afternoon looking as unflappable as ever. Open in front of me on a small podium was a notebook with the pages of bar codes. "I want to talk about Coach Moore's recruiting of players, Mr. Davie. Am I correct that you do not know what his responsibilities were with respect to recruiting?"

Davie confidently deflected the question. "I thought Coach Moore's responsibilities were probably parallel to all the other assistant coaches on the staff at Notre Dame."

"Do you remember when I took your deposition?" Reaching to a small shelf under the podium, I picked up a black remote control, tentatively passed it over one of the bar codes in the notebook, and pushed the button.

Instantly, Davie appeared on the screen, bigger than life, listening intently as my audio voice asked, "Do you know during the time you were at Notre Dame what Coach Moore's responsibility was with respect to recruiting?"

On video, Davie shrugged his shoulders. "I really don't know what his responsibilities were."

In the courtroom I asked Davie, "Has your memory gotten better now in terms of what his responsibilities were from the time I took the deposition?"

When Davie again tried to evade the question, I reached for the video remote. "Maybe we're kind of like ships in the night here. Let me try it one more time and see where we are. . . . You don't know specifically what went on in terms of who recruited the players who were under Coach Moore, do you?"

Davie, eyeing the remote and the blank screen, said, "I don't."

I put the remote down. "So as of November, 1996, Mr. Davie, the time you let Coach Moore go, you did not have a strong opinion one way or the other regarding Coach Moore's recruiting ability; isn't that true?"

"True," he said after a pause. He glanced at the remote again, then volunteered: "Thinking back, I thought he did an excellent job recruiting offensive linemen, that he went out and he did a good job recruiting linemen."

There it was—a direct contradiction between Wadsworth and Beauchamp on the one hand and Davie on the other on the reasons for the termination.

A successful cross-examination can take on momentum much like a football team on a successful drive toward a touchdown. Davie went on to concede the point that he would have kept Moore if he thought Moore would have remained on the staff for five years—a point I intended to use with the judge in arguing for five years of front pay. Davie also acknowledged that when he fired Moore on December 2nd, Davie's concern about continuity—that Moore would not remain for the full five years of the contract—was the only reason that he gave him, and that he never mentioned any other reasons to him.

I asked him whether he had said, "Moore was going to be sixty-five years old in February," and he replied that he "may have mentioned his age not in regard to—" When I interrupted to insist that he answer yes or no, he said that he "may have made that statement, that he was sixty-five years old, in the meeting."

"In fact, you said, in your opinion he's only going to coach another year or two, isn't that what you said?"

"That's accurate."

"And you told those players at the meeting, you said to them you wanted a fresh and new look for the coaching staff; isn't that true?"

"I don't remember making that statement. I know that after—"

I tried to stop him from blunting the impact of this by providing a context: "If you don't remember making the statement—"

"Can I finish?"

Judge Sharp intervened. "Yes, you may finish your answer."

"I don't remember making that statement," he said. "I may have talked about our offense going in a different direction relative to a new, fresh style offense, which may have involved throwing the football a little more."

I brought Davie's deposition to the big screen again:

Q: Did you say you wanted a fresh new look for the coaching staff?

A: I may have said that.

Q: What's your best recollection?

A: My best recollection is I did say that.

Davie had been once again contradicted by his own image. "Does that refresh your recollection?" I asked.

"Yes," he said.

And would he tell the jury the last thing he said to Joe, two days after his discharge?

Intent on avoiding another video display, Davie said, "The last thing I said to Joe Moore was 'fuck you,' and I left."

"So the parting words of Notre Dame, as far as you know, to Coach Moore—" here Hoye objected "—after nine years of service were 'fuck you'; is that correct?"

"That's correct," he said, quietly.

Davie answered my questions about his meeting with Justin Hall as if he wanted to help build a case against Notre Dame. "And at that meeting, it's true, is it not, that you said to Hall about Coach Moore, 'Let's face it; he's sixty-four years old'?"

"That statement is true. I did make that statement to Justin Hall."

I believed it was essential to establish that while Davie professed concern that Joe might retire in a few years, he did not seem to care that younger coaches might leave within the same period of time to pursue other opportunities. Davie acknowledged that Colletto, who was thirteen years younger than Joe, had told him that he might accept another head coach position after "two or three years" at Notre Dame. I asked if it concerned him that his new offensive line coach could possibly be out of there in two or three years.

"No. In fact, I liked that because his goals were to become a head football coach again."

"But it bothered you that Mr. Moore might retire in the next two or three years?"

In connection with this disparity of attitude toward Joe Moore and younger coaches, Davie said that he knew that his new defensive coordinator, Greg Mattison, had a history of moving from school to school every two to three years, but that, in mitigation, each step for Mattison was a move up. But he had to admit that after only three years Mattison had left the University of Michigan, the 1996 national champion, to move to unranked Notre Dame.

Davie also admitted that he had limited knowledge of the spring 1995 and Florida State incidents. He had heard about the Florida incident from a Disney executive during a fifteen-second conversation a full year after it happened. Davie couldn't remember who had told him about the spring 1995 incident. And he had fired Joe without reviewing his personnel file, or seeing the reprimand from Holtz, or even talking to Joe about either incident.

I went through each of the many reasons that Davie had given for firing Joe, in an attempt to discredit them. He said that verbal intimidation of players—particularly the use of words like pussy, coward and asshole—was near the top of his list for firing Joe. But he had to admit that he himself used foul language when he was coaching.

He had also accused Joe of defying authority by arguing with Holtz in front of the players. But on the stand, it developed that Davie had never checked with Holtz to see if he actually disapproved of this. And Joe sometimes did not attend staff meetings, but Davie didn't know whether Holtz had excused him from attending.

I asked Davie whether he had ever told Joe that his smoking bothered him? Or that his dirty office disturbed him? Or that his treatment of his dealer car was a problem? Or that it was not a good idea for his friend to change his clothes at home instead of in the locker room with the other coaches?

Did he mention any of these concerns to anyone at all—the players, Justin Hall, Michael Wadsworth or Father Beauchamp?

In every instance, Davie's answer was "No."

Focusing on Davie's criticism of Joe's performance as an offensive line coach, I asked, when Davie had hired Colletto to take over Joe's job, "was it your intent to get someone to do those duties better?" Davie acknowledged that that certainly was his hope. Then why would he hire Colletto, with his poor record at Purdue?

Davie said it was true that Colletto "didn't have a very good record at Purdue" but he didn't feel that statistics meant everything in college football.

"Just so I understand," I said, "it's your contention that in order to get better performance from the offensive line, you hired a man who was an unsuccessful coach in terms of his records at another school?"

"What do you mean by unsuccessful?"

"Lousy record." Pointing out that under Colletto, Notre Dame's rushing statistics fell from an eighth national ranking during Moore's final year to thirty-sixth, I asked Davie whether this decline had anything to do with the assignment of offensive line coaching to a new coach, leaving Colletto with coordinating duties.

"But you're correct," Davie said. "We didn't run the football nearly as good as we did in the past."

Before concluding, I made another attempt to ask about Davie's conduct at Arizona and Tulane. This annoyed the judge, who sent the jury out of the room.

"I would like to examine Mr. Davie about his definition of defying authority, and this gets into Tulane and Arizona," I said.

"Ninety seconds," said the judge.

"Pardon?"

"I'll give you ninety seconds. That's what I normally give to lawyers when I'm getting ready to rule against them."

I tried to explain quickly that because Davie had a history of serious acts of defying authority—defrauding Arizona, engineering a spying mission and then covering it up—it was not credible that he fired Moore for defying authority over such trivial matters as smoking or not changing in the locker room.

Judge Sharp cut me off. "I'm not going to let you do it."

But it didn't matter to Joe. In the hallway during the break he smiled warmly at me and said, "You destroyed him."

I hoped the day's session would end before Notre Dame began examining Davie. But Judge Sharp was determined to push the case forward. Hoye, who seemed to be taking over the defense, came forward to conduct the examination.

Davie's confidence gradually returned; for the next three hours he provided crisp, well-thought-out responses to Hoye's carefully crafted questions, and his earnest, all-American personality shone brightly through. One could readily see why Wadsworth had telephoned him in late fall of 1996 to inform him in confidence that Lou Holtz might resign, and to ask him whether he would be interested in competing for the head coaching position. Davie was, of course, very interested, and, within days, was invited to be interviewed by a

committee of three at Wadsworth's home. The night before
the interview, Davie carefully wrote out a list of the things
he would want to accomplish if he became head coach of
Notre Dame. And at the interview, Davie gave the committee the essence of his coaching philosophy: "I've got a son at
home, and I don't think you can ever go wrong in coaching
or probably anything, if you follow that guideline right there.
I treat each member of our football team as if he were my
son."

The coaching staff's attitude must change, he said. The
players weren't having fun; the coaches lacked a spirit of
camaraderie. More enthusiasm was needed. "Just enjoying
it more and being more together as a staff, that was number
one," Davie earnestly told the committee. And also on his
list of potential improvements was a stable coaching staff
with minimal turnover: staff continuity, he believed, was
about "family values at Notre Dame," which was "different" and "special." And constant coaching staff turnover
seriously undercut those family values.

Davie's third point to the committee involved "discipline,
but not harassment." There was a fine line between the two;
he felt strongly that the line should never, ever, be crossed.
There are, he said, two types of coaches and two ways of
handling things: "One is negative and wants to tear down,
and the other is positive and wants to bring out the best in
everyone."

This, he told the jury, was his creed, and when he was
appointed head coach several weeks later, he was given the
authority that all head coaches possess: to hire his own assistant football coaches. He had to make a decision about
Joe Moore. And that was not an easy decision because he

liked Joe and believed Joe had "a lot of qualities." However, there were many reasons why he couldn't keep Joe on his staff. Watching him coach over the years, Davie had come to believe that Joe was "abusive by nature." And things that happened while he and Joe worked together at Notre Dame contributed to his conclusion that Joe's style was incompatible with his own.

There was the 1994 Florida State incident that Davie heard about in '95 from a Disney executive, Phil Lengyel. He didn't know all the details, but he did know that Joe tried to punch two players under the face mask on the sidelines, and that Lengyel kept the ABC cameras from televising the incident. During the same game, Joe went after some offensive linemen at halftime and Holtz had to step in and break it up. The following year, Joe took some players into the locker room and "smacked them around" during the spring game. And only weeks before Davie received the head coaching job, he learned that at the game in Ireland, Joe had taken some players into the parking lot at 1:30 in the morning to discipline them. Some Notre Dame fans and people in the hotel saw the incident from their windows and hollered out "to stop it, to stop it, let the kids go." The next day Davie was told by the cheerleaders' advisor that "Joe Moore is a bigger problem than any of those kids."

And there was more, Davie passionately told the jury. Joe used methods that were simply abusive. The mirror-dodge drill he used in practice which forced two players to move back and forth at full speed, mirroring each other for long periods of time, was, Davie said, "abusive to me and also to the players who saw it on defense." Then there was the verbal abuse—calling players "assholes"; telling a religious player, Jerry Wisny, that "you ought to pray for some fucking balls," and other inappropriate comments on the field.

Joe also had his own agenda and simply did not believe in Davie's philosophy of "all for one, one for all." Every day during the season, Joe would leave the office at eleven o'clock and return at two. He never came to the office at night like the other coaches. And "it may seem silly to people, but in three years, Joe Moore never changed clothes and never showered with the coaches in the locker room." It also greatly troubled Davie to see "Joe and Lou arguing on the field in front of players." He felt that it showed a lack of respect for the person in charge. "Football is a team sport and so is coaching, and there's a camaraderie developed by all the things I'm talking about."

At 5:30, Judge Sharp interrupted the testimony and recessed the trial until the next day.

My partner Rick Mason had watched the proceedings that day with his twelve-year-old son, Andrew. I asked Rick what he thought.

"Davie's doing a very effective job now that his lawyer is examining him. He's impressive—I can understand how he got the job."

"You think the jury will believe him?"

"They might. We could lose this," Rick said.

Joe was worried about Davie's testimony, too. He said reluctantly, "I think I'm going to have to get back on the stand to talk about some of the things he raised." Casting around for some positive feedback, I asked Andrew Mason what he thought of the day's events. But the boy simply shrugged his shoulders.

The media was now finding the trial irresistible: there was the spectacle of Notre Dame football players testifying against their head coach; there was Davie's testimony that Joe had abused players—and of course there were the cheerleaders having sex, virtually in public. On the third morning of the trial, the courtroom was filled with reporters. One said that it was more difficult to get a seat in the courtroom than at a Notre Dame football game.

Davie resumed the stand and his earnest litany of reasons for the firing: Joe smoked constantly—at practices, during games, and at coaches' meetings—in violation of the rules. During staff meetings he would simply sit and doodle without taking notes. He was so disorganized that Holtz had become frustrated with him and during the 1996 season had coached the offensive tackles himself.

As to continuity, Joe had openly told Davie and other staff members that he was probably only going to coach for another year, saying, "You guys are crazy for doing this. A year from now I'll be golfing and you guys will still be at it." This, Davie said, did affect his decision to let Joe go, but that decision had absolutely nothing to do with Joe's age; he was motivated solely by Joe's expressed intention to quit in the near future.

Hoye paused and, looking meaningfully at Davie, said gravely, "Coach Davie, I would like you to turn and face this jury and tell them whether your decision not to hire Coach Moore had anything whatsoever to do with his age."

Davie swiveled slowly in his chair to look into the eyes of each juror, and said emphatically, "Age had nothing to do with me not hiring Joe Moore."

He denied that he ever discussed Joe's age or retirement plans with Earl Mosley. And while he may have mentioned Joe's age to the players, it was only in the context of telling them that Joe was just going to coach another year or two. As to the December 2nd meeting at Joe's apartment, before Davie could tell him why he was firing him, Joe interrupted to say that he planned to coach only another year or two. It was true that Davie told Justin Hall, "Christ, let's face it; he's going to be sixty-five years old"—but that was only an expression of frustration because Joe's age had been discussed in connection with his contract.

When Hoye finished, I stood up to face a very confident Coach Davie. Somehow, I thought, I had to bring him back to where my examination had left him yesterday. It wouldn't be easy; he was an athlete: if he lost one day, he shook it off and started all over the next day.

During his deposition a year before, Davie had inadvertently mentioned his personal feelings toward Lou Holtz. I never thought that I would have an opportunity to use those comments at trial, but Davie had provided an opening.

"Now, on cross," I told him, "you said one of the reasons that you let Coach Moore go was that he failed to show respect in front of Coach Holtz and in front of the players; is that not correct?"

He answered positively, "In my opinion, he repeatedly did that, yes."

"And isn't it correct that you yourself showed a lack of respect for Coach Holtz in talking to another coach?"

He immediately became defensive. "I never did that repeatedly, if that happened. None of us are perfect." When I began to leaf through my bar code notebook, he added, "I may have said something."

"You told another coach that you hated and despised things about Coach Holtz, didn't you? Was that showing respect for Coach Holtz? Let me ask you—"

Judge Sharp interrupted. "One question at a time."

Davie sat ramrod straight. "I believe I did say there were things about—things that Lou Holtz did that I hated and despised. That's an accurate statement. I had a lot of respect for Lou Holtz, but there were certain things that I despised that he did."

"And you consider that, sir, the kind of camaraderie and positive actions by coaches with respect to their boss?"

"I said what I believed at that time in a private conversation with Joe Moore."

"In fact, didn't you on another occasion to Coach Moore speculate as to whether Holtz was having mental problems?"

"At the end of the '96 season, there were some things that happened that I was concerned about. Yes, I made that statement with Joe Moore in a private conversation."

"You consider that it is respectful to say to another coach that you think your boss is having mental problems? Is that the kind of respect you were looking for in terms of hiring new coaches, sir?"

Judge Sharp interrupted. "Save your argument until the end."

Standing a few feet from Davie, I could sense the rapt attention of the audience behind me. Those who were attending for the first time, drawn in by the preceding day's newspaper coverage, were not disappointed by what they were hearing; Davie's questioning Holtz's sanity would be considered blasphemous by any Notre Dame football fan.

I asked, "When you made your presentation for your new job, you talked about how you should do positive things for punishments like sending the kids out to do charities and so on?" And was that was his "true and sincere belief?" Yes, he believed that discipline should be imposed only in constructive ways like study halls and community service.

"Now, in the spring of 1997, isn't it true that two of your players got in a fight—Malcolm Johnson and Joe Thomas?"

"I wouldn't call it a fight, but they squared off and swung at each other, yeah."

"Thomas swung at Johnson and one of these guys broke his hand. You don't call that a fight?"

"Yeah. We found out later that when he took the swing, he broke a bone in his hand, yeah."

"Did you realize these guys were having a fight?"

"Yes."

"And in order to deal with this situation, isn't it true that you lined these two guys up on the line, helmet to helmet, to settle their differences. You blew your whistle and said 'Go,' and they hit each other over and over and over and over again—two, three or four times. That's what you did, Mr. Davie, did you not, to discipline these guys for having a fight?"

Davie snapped back, "That's exactly what I did."

"That's true, that's exactly what you did."

"That's exactly what I did," Davie repeated, and started to go on, but I interrupted him. "Thank you. I'll go on to the next question."

He protested. "That's what football is, blocking."

I nodded. "That's exactly what football is. It's a tough game, isn't it? The truth is, is it not, if you were teaching these guys anything, you were teaching them toughness, not football skills?"

"I was teaching them they shouldn't fight on the football field. I see nothing wrong with that. We haven't had any fights since."

"I think we agree with you."

I went on with him for another twenty minutes. When Hoye waived further examination, Davie was excused and Judge Sharp called a short recess. Satisfied with the examination but relieved that it was over, I walked through the clusters of reporters and spectators to the men's room at the far end of the hallway. Davie was standing at the urinal. Weighing my options, I decided I had no real choice but to walk to the adjacent urinal. We stood silently side by side; when Davie walked to the sink to wash, he was smiling. "I don't know how you guys remember all that information," he said. "It's just amazing to me."

After a moment I realized that he was referring to his deposition. "Well," I said, "it's just what we do. I could never remember all those Xs and Os. I don't even know what they mean."

He left the room, still smiling and shaking his head.

The final two bricks in our wall were the two men who had replaced Joe: Jim Colletto and Dave Borberly, the thirty-eight-year-old youthful-looking offensive line coach recently hired for the next season.

Colletto, amiable as before, readily acknowledged that he was an intense, aggressive coach who created an unpleasant environment in practice so that players would learn to survive, and that he sometimes engaged in extreme behavior in order to make a point to his players. For example, once at Purdue, meeting with the players in the locker room, he lost his temper, picked up a chair and smashed it into a pillar. A piece of the chair ricocheted into a player, injuring him. At Notre Dame, he didn't change his style. The preceding season, in a halftime session in the locker room with Davie present, Colletto screamed at the players and knocked over a blackboard with his hand. He stopped in the midst of this cursing rampage when he noticed Father Beauchamp in a corner of the room.

This was helpful testimony, but I needed to bring out evidence of the Ryan Harmon lawsuit. With the jury absent, I pleaded with Judge Sharp to let me question Colletto about it. To my relief, the judge said he would allow some questions, although he didn't know how far he would let it go.

In response to my questions and consistent with his deposition testimony, Colletto denied that he had physically attacked Harmon. Then I moved into the heart of the matter: Colletto's acknowledgment during his deposition that Michael Wadsworth and Bob Davie knew about the Harmon lawsuit when Colletto was interviewed at Notre Dame in December, 1996. Over Hoye's objections, Judge Sharp permitted me to ask whether his dealings with players at Purdue were discussed during his Notre Dame interview. Colletto said no, they weren't discussed.

When I began to read Colletto's deposition testimony describing his discussion of the Harmon case during the job interview, the judge cut me off. "No," he said, "I'm not going to let you do this."

Despite this, the Colletto examination went better than I expected. Judge Sharp allowed just enough questioning about the Harmon matter to let the jury understand that there had been a disturbing incident in Colletto's past and that Notre Dame knew about it before they hired him. Then too, some of the jurors could have read about the Harmon case in the Lafayette newspapers. So I felt that I may have accomplished two things with Colletto: brought the Harmon matter to the jury's attention, and, if the case was lost, created reversible error based on Judge Sharp's constraints on my questioning. The judge was in error, I believed, because a crucially important part of our case was the inconsistency between Notre Dame's claim that they fired Joe for being abusive while they immediately hired Colletto, who had been accused of similar, if not more serious, behavior. So the judge's limitations prejudiced us in presenting our case to the jury.

Before Judge Sharp recessed for the weekend, he asked Notre Dame whom they were calling as witnesses. Lutkus listed a dozen people, including assistant coaches, three players, and James Russ, the team's head athletic trainer and physical therapist. Mimi objected: some of these men had not been deposed before trial.

"No witness testifies in my trials unless the other side has an opportunity to depose him," Judge Sharp said. "If you want to call these witnesses, make them available to Mr. Moore's lawyers before we reconvene on Tuesday morning."

Lutkus said that he would phone us over the weekend to make arrangements for the depositions.

Back in Chicago that evening, I picked up my daughter Claire, who had been staying with friends; my wife Tina was at our cottage for the weekend. Claire wanted to get home, but I insisted that we stop somewhere and look at early editions of the Sunday papers. At the local Walgreen's, we leafed through the bulky papers, looking for something on the case.

"Wow, Dad, look at this!" Claire pointed to a full page in the *Chicago Sun-Times* headed "Trial Bombshell Embarrasses Irish." Standing in the drugstore, we read the page together. One story, "Current Irish Coach Admits Concern About Predecessor," documented Davie's disrespectful feelings about Lou Holtz, and reported that Holtz's wife Beth had spent much of the day taking calls for her husband from the national press. But it was the companion column by Jay Mariotti that drew our attention:

> Used to be Touchdown Jesus was the symbol of Notre Dame football. Now it's either Jerry Springer or Judge Wapner, pick your trash TV. And forget about seeing that gleaming vision from the toll road, a golden dome. It's too caked with mud now.
>
> You can't help but smirk about the demise of the Litigating Irish. All these years, they've refused to let us look inside their inner sanctum, and now that door finally is opened by a landmark lawsuit, we see a petty family rife with vicious backstabbing, alleged violence, skeletons and enough dirt to fill the *National Enquirer*.

This is a saga that could take down Notre Dame as we know it. We've always been led to believe the program is beyond reproach, holy and blessed by gods, a mighty monolith, glorified in Hollywood and furthered by NBC's wealth. But after two days of testimony in a U.S. District courtroom in Lafayette, Ind., it's obvious the pious Domers are no different than any other money-hoarding collegiate machine.

Jeer, jeer for old Notre shame.

No matter who wins the case, an image loses in a rout.

"Wow, Dad!" Claire repeated.

I anticipated a grueling week dealing with Notre Dame's defense witnesses, but my first priority was preparing the closing argument. Through Saturday evening into the early hours of Sunday morning, I scribbled points, ideas and partial paragraphs, but I couldn't seem to organize a coherent argument. Wound up from the long day, I slept poorly and woke early to a perfect July morning. I drove to the beach, not too far from my house, and rented a small sailboat. As I worked the sails, trying to capture the elusive breeze, I forgot about the case and began to relax. Soon a steady wind came up, and as I sailed along, the closing argument began to take shape in my mind.

That afternoon, Tina came home and volunteered to be my sounding board. I had organized my random thoughts into a series of "talking points," and as I read, she expressed her approval or disapproval of each one. All afternoon I wrote and rewrote the points, asking her, after each revision, what she thought. Later in the evening she said, "Well, I'm convinced. You should go to bed."

Joe and Fran stayed in their hotel room in Lafayette over the weekend, trying to relax, but they kept getting supportive phone calls from family and friends. John Patrick, their seventeen-year-old grandson, phoned several times. Following the case closely in the newspapers and on the Internet, he was upset by the accusations of abuse against Joe. "Is what they're saying about Grandpa true?" he kept asking Fran.

Fran tried to shield Joe from these calls, but he understood better than anyone that if he lost the case, the professional accomplishments he had spent a lifetime building, would be destroyed. If the jury found against him, he knew he would be remembered only as the abusive, bitter coach who had unsuccessfully sued Notre Dame.

On Sunday, Notre Dame told us that they were dropping from their witness list everyone who had not been deposed except for the athletic trainer James Russ, who would be available for deposition in Lafayette on Monday afternoon, and would be called as a witness when the trial resumed on Tuesday. On Monday morning, Mimi scrambled to find a court reporter who could take the deposition and transcribe the testimony before court on Tuesday. Every court reporting service in the area declined; it was only after Mimi pleaded in desperation, that a reporter agreed to do it.

Joe was worried about Russ. Seven years earlier, in the middle of a game, Russ had told Joe's offensive linemen that the team would lose its quarterback if they didn't do a better job of blocking. Joe ordered him to get away from the players and mind his own business. When Lou Holtz heard about this, he had asked Joe if he wanted Russ fired, but Joe did not want to go that far. Even though Joe had saved Russ's job, Russ had reason to hold a grudge against him.

Joe gave Mimi a list of questions. "Mimi, the most important thing to ask him is whether I ever played an injured player. There's just no way he could say that."

But at his deposition in the hotel conference room, Russ said exactly that—that Joe, repeatedly ignoring medical restrictions, forced injured players to participate in practices and games. Joe could barely restrain himself as Russ testified that Joe instructed players with second degree ankle sprains to hop up and down to determine their condition, and ordered athletes with shoulder or knee injuries to play. Through the interminable afternoon, Joe glared at Russ, shook his head in disbelief and whispered urgent suggestions to Mimi. But it was notable that while Russ was able to give detailed descriptions of Joe's conduct, he couldn't seem to recall names of the players or dates of the occurrences.

"Can you give me an example?" Mimi asked.

"I don't know whether I can give you an example. Well, you're asking nine years of a history of who had contact, who was limited, who should not do this, who should not do that. And that's very difficult to answer specifically as you want it."

"I just want one example."

Finally, he mentioned two incidents; he didn't have firsthand knowledge of either one: Mike Rosenthal had sprained his ankle, and Jeremy Akers had injured his knee. He admitted that he knew of other Notre Dame coaches who made their athletes play without medical clearance.

"Which position coaches were those?"

"I'm—I can't give you names. I won't give you names."

"You are going to refuse to answer the question?"

"No. I answered the question. I don't remember names. But I don't—this is not about them."

With each question, Russ became increasingly unwilling or unable to recall any details. Finally, when Mimi asked if Notre Dame kept medical records of players' injuries, Russ reluctantly replied that doctors, staff members and he himself kept track of every athlete's injury and illness. These extensive records, dating back to the 1950s, were filed in his office.

Mimi turned to Lutkus. "Jerry, I know it's late in the game to make a request for these records, but if Mr. Russ is going to be testifying about the injuries of these players, then we want those records."

When the deposition ended, and Russ and Lutkus left, the court reporter said to Mimi, "If you had told me that this was the famous case that's been on television every day, I wouldn't have given you a hard time about doing this."

That evening, as Mimi was working at the desk in her room, making notes of questions to put to Russ the next day, she was interrupted by a knock on the door. She looked at her watch, and was surprised to see that it was 4:30 in the morning. She opened the door to the court reporter delivering the completed transcript.

At 7:30 A.M. Bill Wortel phoned Mimi to tell her that he found a flashing message light on his phone when he woke up: Notre Dame had decided not to call Russ as a witness.

On Tuesday morning the Notre Dame witness list had dwindled to five. Their leading witness was Phil Lengyel, vice president of sports for Walt Disney World, who had watched fourteen Notre Dame games from the sidelines as a guest of Lou Holtz. His deposition had been videotaped and was now played for the jury.

Lengyel testified that at every single game, he had been appalled by Coach Moore's "unbelievably vitriolic" treatment of the players, and shocked by his "spewing of obscenities" and "relentless verbal abuse"—calling them "you fucking idiots and you fucking embarrassments"—and slamming and even throwing his portable chalkboard. His most outrageous behavior occurred at the 1994 Florida State game, when he was apparently furious at the poor performance of the offensive line during the first half. In one particularly unsettling incident, Lengyel observed, "the coach put his hand up into the helmet of a player named Chris Clevenger and begin to shake his fist with his hand on the face mask, punching Clevenger in the face to the point where blood was noticed, while yelling and screaming at him the whole time." During halftime in the locker room, Lengyel said he saw the coach get so angry that "Coach Holtz from some distance away had to walk over and restrain Coach Moore."

When Mimi cross-examined him, also on video, Lengyel admitted that despite his long friendship with Lou Holtz, George Kelly and later with Michael Wadsworth, he had never told any of them about Moore's behavior, even though he and Lou Holtz frequently played golf and had dinner together. In fact, he never said a word about Coach Moore until he read about the lawsuit in the newspapers, when he decided to volunteer to testify for Notre Dame.

I thought Mimi's cross-examination raised serious doubts about Lengyel's impartiality. Joe, who had not seen the video before, was understandably upset by his testimony. He kept repeating, "This guy is killing us." During the break, he steered me through the crowded corridors away from the crowd into a tiny stairwell, and urgently asked me, "What happens if we lose?"

"Joe, if we lose, we'll appeal."

"Can we win an appeal?"

"I think the judge committed reversible error by keeping out the Colletto stuff."

Agitated, he said, "I just want to know, do we have a chance to win? My grandson called and asked if I had done all those things that they said in the papers. I don't want to let him down."

"You won't."

"I can't. I love him."

Notre Dame's defense was over in less than a day. We didn't know whether they had decided to drop so many scheduled witnesses because of difficulties in making them available at the last minute, or because they thought their testimony might not be effective, or—as I tended to believe—because they wanted to end the case quickly to cut off the publicity. The trial was getting national daily coverage in newspapers and on talk radio. One caller in Chicago remarked that the only ones who improved their image as a result of the trial were the male Notre Dame cheerleaders.

Lou Holtz, after several days of silence, issued a lengthy press release noting that he was "completely mystified" and "confounded" by Davie's remarks about him in court.

The *Chicago Tribune* commented, "This trial is about figurative knives stuck in the backs by the adults in charge. This downfall involves a coaching staff that apparently has been too busy playing political football to concentrate on recruiting stars and winning games. Call them the Infighting Irish. How about Touchdown Judas?"

For the first time, the jurors seemed bored by the witnesses. One juror fell asleep. Two coaches testified that Joe told them he might leave coaching within a few years, but they also said, on cross-examination, that Davie never asked them for a commitment to stay with the program for any length of time, and that Davie understood that they might well leave if they got a better offer elsewhere.

The former Cornell head coach testified that Joe had verbally accepted a $40,000 offer to coach their offensive line but backed out when he couldn't find suitable housing. Notre Dame's point here was that since Joe had walked away from the Cornell job, his recoverable damages should be minimal.

After Notre Dame rested its case, Mimi announced that Joe would testify as a rebuttal witness. This annoyed Judge Sharp, who had thought the case was over. Mimi wanted Joe to respond to Davie's litany of reasons for firing him, but she ran into trouble at the outset when she asked Joe, "With respect to Mr. Davie's criticism of how you treated players, what, if anything did you do to help the players?"

Lutkus objected.

"Objection sustained. This is rebuttal," said Judge Sharp.

"Your Honor, Mr. Davie proffered this as a reason—Coach Moore's treatment of players."

"I have ruled, Counsel. I have a lot of discretion at this point, and I'm exercising it tightly, so get on."

She tried again. "Coach Moore, did players ever come to you for help in any way?"

Lutkus objected.

"No, that's far afield from what . . . the trial is almost over. The objection is sustained," Judge Sharp ruled.

After that, Lutkus objected to virtually every question, and the judge sustained the objections. At one point I protested that Moore was simply responding to Davie's accusations—which is proper rebuttal. The judge motioned me to sit down. "You're not involved in this! It's one lawyer at a time, and it's this lawyer right here."

Mimi calmly continued working her way through her list of questions. After a while the judge began to overrule the constant objections, and to permit Joe to answer "in the interest of caution."

When he finally had the opportunity to do it, Joe answered fully and thoughtfully. About his being disrespectful to Coach Holtz, Joe told the jury that Holtz had "a tremendous football mind, and I thought he respected my football mind." He said they had a special relationship and that Holtz often asked his opinion. Sometimes they would "holler" at each other, but that was how they related to each other and in the end, Joe would do whatever Holtz decided.

Mimi asked Joe to demonstrate for the jury those drills that Davie had said were abusive. Standing in the middle of the courtroom, with Bill Wortel acting as an offensive line-man, Joe acted out the mirror-dodge drill while the jury watched intently. "The name of it tells you what it is. It is the same as if you are looking in the mirror; you would hope your reflection would be directly in front of you. So we call it a mirror. Whatever he does," Joe said as Bill shifted from side to side, "I want to mirror him." The two slid back and forth across the courtroom floor as Joe explained the proce-dure, saying this drill was harmless; he often used it with high school players. Typically two kids would practice the drill while the others watched, and then two more would follow. "My theory of coaching is that football is a game of spurts and rest."

"Coach Moore, did Coach Holtz ever tell you not to use either of those two drills?" asked Mimi.

"No."

Lutkus objected.

The judge responded, "He said no! It's in, and I'll leave it in."

Mimi asked whether Joe had ever said that he intended to retire. Lutkus objected, and the judge overruled him.

"Everybody was frustrated at that time, from Coach Holtz down," Joe testified. "He was under pressure. He felt he was being run out of the job, and the people just didn't know what was going on. And people said they were going to do this and they were going to do that. I said various things at various days, but I never had any intention to re-tire. I loved Notre Dame. There was no reason for me to ever want to leave Notre Dame. So the answer is that I never, ever said I was going to retire."

Asked about the spring 1995 episode in the locker room, Joe slowly shook his head, and said that after that game, he never again treated any student athlete inappropriately. "I made a mistake that not only affected me, it affected the kids; it affected my family. No matter what, something like that will never happen again. It was a tragic thing that I did. It's just something you know you've got to live with and make sure it doesn't happen again."

When Mimi finished taking Joe's testimony, I hoped that it would look to the jury as if a judge and a high-powered lawyer had been ganging up on a fragile but determined little woman who was trying to help an honest man bravely defend himself against the accusations of an arrogant institution. When the judge called a recess, one of my partners who had come to Lafayette to watch the proceedings, came up behind me at counsel time and whispered in my ear, "That was awesome."

The day ended with the jury instruction conference which is held in open court between the lawyers and the judge. The purpose of the conference is for the judge to develop a final set of instructions that the jury must follow in deciding the case. Both sides had previously submitted their proposals for instructions. In this case, as in most lawsuits, the final instructions could be so detailed and complex that the jurors might well disregard them and apply their own common sense in deciding the case. So on Tuesday afternoon there were two sets of proposed instructions that could have a real effect on the outcome of the case.

Shortly before the conference, the judge gave the lawyers his own set of instructions and invited them to comment. As Mimi, Bill and I hurriedly reviewed them, we stopped at Court's Instruction No. 23. Instead of limiting the jury's consideration to Joe's lost wages from the time of his termination to the time of the trial, the judge's instruction empowered the jury to award compensatory damages, covering emotional pain and suffering, inconvenience, mental anguish and lost future earnings. This instruction would permit the jury to award whatever damages they wished, with no limit. "This is unbelievable," I kept repeating.

When the conference started, John LaDue objected vehemently to Instruction No. 23. The Age Discrimination in Employment Act, he argued, did not permit such compensatory damages; rather, damages are limited to back pay which the jury may double if they find the violation is willful. Judge Sharp said LaDue was confused, and asked us for our position. Being careful not to misstate the law, I said that I was satisfied with the instruction and had no objection. The judge, who had expected me to provide legal support for the instruction, was not happy with my answer. He finally had to acknowledge that he had made a mistake; he substituted a back pay instruction. My heart sank. "I should know better than to believe in miracles, but for a moment I thought we had a chance to get a million dollars from this jury," I whispered to Bill. Joe, sitting next to him, didn't care. All he worried about was the terrifying possibility of losing the case.

Judge Sharp asked about our Proposed Jury Instruction No. 16, entitled "Continuity—Discriminatory Reason." We wanted an instruction that it was unlawful to discharge older employees based on the assumption that they will work only for a short time: "Put another way, an employer's desire for continuity amongst its personnel is not a legitimate reason for discharging an older employee if that desire is premised on the employer's belief that the employee will soon retire," the proposed instruction read. "Thus, if you find that the defendant's stated reason for terminating plaintiff—continuity—was unlawfully motivated by the stigmatization that older workers are likely to work only a short time, you should enter a verdict for the plaintiff."

LaDue heatedly objected to this instruction on continuity, arguing that it did not represent the law and was misleading and prejudicial. Mimi was prepared. She had located three cases discussing continuity: two supported the instructions and one did not. Judge Sharp asked to see the cases, Mimi handed him the two helpful precedents, and he quickly read them. One, *EEOC v. Community Unit School District No. 9*, involved two school administrators who were demoted after they told their supervisors they intended to retire the following school year. The school district said the demotions were necessary so they could replace the two administrators as soon as possible, in order to preserve continuity. The court in that case ruled that such motivation is evidence of age discrimination because retirement is so closely linked with age.

After reading the decision, Judge Sharp looked at the Notre Dame lawyers. "Do you have any contrary authority?" Mimi held her breath.

"No, Your Honor," said LaDue. The judge said that he was going to adopt at least part of the proposed continuity instruction.

Growing up in a Jewish extended family, I had attended countless weddings, bar mitzvahs and funerals in various cities. Family—cousins, aunts, uncles, distant relatives— would stay in one hotel, socializing at buffet tables, visiting with one another. The night before closing arguments at the Homewood Suites hotel reminded me of those family gatherings, but I couldn't decide whether it felt like the evening before a funeral or a bar mitzvah.

In the late afternoon, after working in my room to refine the closing argument, I went to the buffet in the hotel lobby, where I found Judge Sharp filling his plate. He chatted amiably, asking whether I knew some of his lawyer friends in Chicago. Later in the evening, I visited the suite that served as our team's war room. Surrounded by stacks of papers, files, boxes, videotapes, computer equipment and food, sat Mimi, Bill Wortel, and my partners Rick Mason and Tim Klenk, who had driven down to hear closing arguments.

As we discussed our worries about the case, Rick interjected a positive note: his twelve-year-old son Andrew, who had heard Davie's testimony, hadn't said much at the time. But on the drive home to Chicago, when Rick pressed him for his opinion, he answered as if it was obvious, "Oh, Coach Moore will win. Davie's a big liar." I took some comfort from that, but, on the whole, everyone thought that winning or losing hung on closing arguments.

I read my argument to them and made whatever changes we all agreed were needed. In the lobby, on my way to the gift shop to buy a candy bar, I passed Davie and Michael Wadsworth sitting at a table engaged in intense conversation. We glanced at each other, and looked away.

I met Gerald Lutkus on the way back to my room. He didn't seem to have a care in the world, and was more friendly than I had ever seen him. "It's been an interesting experience the last few days," he said, "fighting a two-front war—in court and in the media." He seems so relaxed, I thought, that he must be taking Valium—or someone else is giving their closing argument. Joe had suggested that Lutkus had been demoted; maybe he was right.

The only people missing from this movable feast were the Moores. Exhausted, Joe had gone to bed early, leaving Fran to field the onslaught of telephone calls from family and friends.

The following morning, we arrived at the courthouse to find two television trucks with giant portable satellite dishes parked on the corner, and to face a firing squad of five video cameramen. The courtroom was standing room only, packed with reporters, including Lester Munson, the *Sports Illustrated* writer who had put the case back into the national spotlight.

As I stood facing them, the eight jurors stared at me with rapt attention. Most of them were taking their responsibilities with the utmost seriousness. They want to render the right verdict, I thought, but they need a factual and legal road map, and I was determined to give them one.

"Mr. Lieberman." The judge nodded at me.

I began, somewhat stiffly, by explaining that age discrimination laws are no different from race, sex, or national origin laws: an employer cannot rely upon such basic characteristics in making employment decisions.

"When we talk about age, what does that mean?" I asked. "It's really more than just the individual's chronological age. It's the employer's feeling or belief or even knowledge that in the future an older person is going to have diminished performance. It's the employer's feeling that they don't want anyone around who looks old. The feeling that in my restaurant or on my football field, I want young-looking people, because they show us off better than the people who look aged. It's the employer's feeling or knowledge that if you hire older persons, they are more likely to leave earlier than younger persons because they're going to die sooner or retire sooner.

"That's all illegal! It's illegal for the employer to think that 'I'm not going to have older people because they're going to retire.' As people get older, virtually everybody retires and virtually everybody talks about retirement. They may mention it to their colleagues or they may attend retirement seminars at their company. It is illegal for an employer to fire somebody or not hire somebody because that person will retire in the future.

"It's very much like employment discrimination with respect to women where they are looking to have a family; and, as a result, the company feels they may leave the job. An employer cannot fire a woman or refuse to hire a woman based on the belief that if we bring on this lady or we keep her in the organization, she may have a baby."

Then I tackled my biggest concern—that the jury would decide that Joe should have been fired regardless of what Davie's actual motivation was. "It's not the jury's job to decide whether you think the person should be fired. The only

issue is really whether Mr. Davie was motivated in part—
whether one of the motivating reasons by Mr. Davie in terms
of firing Joe Moore—was his age. It's not about coming in
and second guessing what you would have done if you were
in that place. This is, I think, particularly important in this
case, because we heard this laundry list of reasons that Mr.
Davie talked about that came up after Joe Moore was told
he was fired. But the issue is Mr. Davie's reason at the time
he thought about this and then fired Joe Moore. This is not
about something he came up with later, and said this would
have been a good idea or that would have been a good idea."

Did I still have their attention? All eight were still staring
at me. "What is the evidence of age discrimination in this
case?" We had hung a huge chart that detailed, chronologi-
cally, Davie's age-related statements. I wanted the jury to see
how all the pieces came together, like a jigsaw puzzle.

"Everything happened within a real tight time frame," I
said, pointing to the first item on the chart: Davie's appointment as head coach in November. The second entry on the
chart was Davie's comment about Joe to Earl Mosley a few
days later. I paused and asked Judge Sharp for permission to
show Mosley's testimony on this to the jury.

Instantly, Mosley's larger-then-life image loomed on the
screen, saying, "Mr. Davie asked me how old Coach Moore
was. I responded to that, I think sixty-four or sixty-five, and
the second question he asked me was how long did I think
he was going to coach, and I responded I didn't know. I said
Coach Moore is a football coach. He'll coach forever in the
right situation."

I watched the jury as the jury watched Mosley. They
seemed transfixed. This is magic, I thought, and immedi-

ately decided to use these videotapes as my closing argument, and simply comment on them as if I were watching television with friends.

I said conversationally, "Now, you might remember that Mr. Davie said that that conversation with Mosley never occurred. He absolutely, totally, denied it. Why did he deny it? Because it's so incriminating that if he admitted it, he would have to admit that age was a motivating factor in terms of firing Mr. Moore." At this point, I showed Mosley testifying that Davie had asked him how old he was: "Of course, Mr. Davie denied that too."

Reviewing the December 2nd conversation between Joe and Davie in Joe's living room, I said, "Again, Mr. Davie basically denies this conversation. So at this point Mr. Davie is saying that Mr. Mosley is a liar, that Coach Moore is a liar, and that Mrs. Moore is a liar as well."

Next on the chart came Davie's meeting with the players the same afternoon, where, I pointed out, we begin to get admissions from Davie for the first time, because he couldn't deny what he said before so many witnesses. "He admitted he said to the players that in his opinion, Joe Moore was only going to coach another year or two and then retire, in his opinion. That's exactly what both Joe Moore and Fran Moore said that he said to them—exactly—and that he denied."

I noted further that on the stand, Davie did try to deny some of the more damning comments that he made to the players, but "when I showed him his videotape, it totally contradicted his testimony." Davie appeared on the screen admitting that he said he wanted "a fresh and new look for the coaching staff." The message Davie conveyed to those

players was "loud and clear—that Coach Moore was old
and that that was the reason." True, each player had a slightly
different recollection—no one remembers things the same
way—but "they all heard what Mr. Davie said."

I reminded the jury that Mike Rosenthal, now captain of
the football team, was not "a flaky kid" but "a responsible
young adult," who earnestly stated, "I remember him saying Coach Moore's age." And there was Chris Clevenger,
who testified on the screen: "He did say, you know, Coach
Moore's old, and I'm looking for a long-term commitment."

Rick Kaczenski's screened deposition testimony followed,
and then a video blowup of Jon Spickelmier's affidavit: "He
wanted to start the program with younger coaches." The
Notre Dame lawyers were going through their papers and
conferring in whispers; they were obviously preparing to
challenge my showing an inadmissible affidavit to the jury.
But their activity stopped, as I knew it would, when they
discovered that they had inadvertently offered the affidavit
as their own exhibit, and realized that we had taken advan-
tage of their mistake.

I continued the chronology: Moore confronted Davie
about retirement talk, asking Davie, "Just tell them you fired
me." And I said, "Coach Davie did tell the truth later that
day when he talked to Justin Hall, the graduate assistant
coach. Justin Hall testified that Davie said one and only one
thing in the terms of the reason: 'Christ, let's face it; he's
sixty-four years old.' Davie said, 'I really can't say why I
said that. I was frustrated.' That was a very telling comment. Why was he frustrated? He was frustrated because he
believed at that age Coach Moore was too old and should

just get out of the way. He was frustrated because he couldn't believe that somebody at that age was fighting to hang on. 'Christ, let's face it; he's sixty-four years old.'"

Age, I reminded them, is an illegal reason for termination, and it was the only reason Davie mentioned. "He did not say to any of these people that there was an issue about Joe's smoking or mistreatment of players or he was a lousy coach or had a dirty car or he was unorganized. Or, "if he wanted to avoid hurting Mr. Moore's feelings, he could have very easily said, 'Well, I let him go because we had a different coaching philosophy or a different style.' He didn't even say that. He expressed himself very, very clearly in terms of the only reason: age, age—the motivating reason." There was no evidence of any other motivation.

I went on to emphasize that Moore and Davie met nearly every day during the season, that they were friends who talked about everything, and that by his own admission Davie never gave Moore other reasons for the firing. "Does that make sense? You'd think, to his buddy he would have said, 'Hey, Joe, you shouldn't cut out of these staff meetings like that,' or 'I really wish you were around at lunch,' or 'What happened with those players two seasons ago back in May of 1995?' and 'You know, people are talking about that.'" But Davie said absolutely nothing about these things, never mentioning them to Earl Mosley, to the players, the graduate assistants, or to his superiors, Michael Wadsworth, Father Beauchamp, Kelly—all these people testified that he never said a word to them about these "reasons." "Never! . . . the first time Mr. Moore ever heard the 'reasons' from Mr. Davie was at Davie's deposition in July of 1997, eight months later."

Where, I asked, did these 'reasons' come from, and how were they developed? "Mr. Wadsworth testified that in December of 1996, right after this happened . . . before any lawyers were involved . . . that he understood that Mr. Moore was raising complaints . . . of age discrimination. Mr. Moore hadn't even said age discrimination at that point, but Mr. Wadsworth understood clearly that the issue was the concern that Davie had fired this long-term employee because of his age. Mr. Wadsworth said that Notre Dame has a policy against age discrimination. He knew that age discrimination was illegal under the law.

"So what did he do? What would any responsible employer do in that situation? Call the employee into his office and say, 'Gee, I hear you're upset about something.' Joe was still working there and this was within days of his termination. What happened? Wadsworth didn't do that. He didn't talk to the players, didn't do any kind of investigation, didn't ask what was said. You heard what he said. He said, 'I went directly to my lawyers.' He left Joe to twist in the wind. He went to his lawyers."

I stopped to catch my breath. The jury was still with me and I felt that I was on a roll, speaking without notes, highlighting undeniable points.

Next, I tackled Notre Dame's "laundry list of reasons" for the firing and the inconsistencies and contradictions that cropped up there: Michael Wadsworth and Father Beauchamp said that Davie told them he fired Moore solely because he was a poor recruiter; but in his deposition—shown on the screen—Davie said he didn't know anything about Moore's recruiting work, and on the stand Davie had admitted that recruiting was not one of the reasons for the firing, and that he had never told anyone that it was. "He couldn't keep his story straight. He got it screwed up and he got caught."

I moved then to our Achilles heel: player mistreatment during the spring 1995 and the fall 1994 games. If, I asked, this behavior was so important to Notre Dame, why wasn't Joe fired at that time? And then why did Davie hire Colletto—a man who used foul language, smashed furniture, even with Davie quietly looking on. I reminded them that during halftime of the Pittsburgh game, Colletto smashed a blackboard and ranted at the players, using language so foul that he had to stop when he noticed that Father Beauchamp was in the room.

And there was Davie's own conduct toward the players: when two of them got into a fight during practice, Davie could have imposed charity work or some similar penalty. But he chose to line them up, blow his whistle and let them smash at each other over and over again. And Phil Lengyel, the Disney witness who testified that he was upset by Moore's abusive behavior, never said a word about it to his friend Lou Holtz when they were golfing and dining together.

Notre Dame argued that Joe had often said he would retire within a year or two, and that Davie simply took him at his word. That, I said, was age discrimination. If you could fire somebody for thinking or talking about retirement, you could get rid of every older person in a work force. This talk of "continuity" was simply disguised age discrimination, and even here Davie employed a double standard: the younger coaches—like Assistant Coach Strong and Jim Colletto—made it perfectly clear that they would leave as soon as they got a better job; there was no commitment from them. Davie knew that coaches move from job to job to job—that obviously didn't bother him with younger men. But he fired someone older because he might retire or even because he might have said he would retire in the future. "That," I said, "is illegal."

Finally, I came to damages. I was limited to asking the jury for back pay covering the short period since the termination; under the age discrimination law, future pay or reinstatement was up to the judge. I used a chart to demonstrate that with salary, bowl bonus and pension contributions, Joe earned $107,000 a year. After deducting his annual earnings from work with the Baltimore Ravens and Cathedral Prep High School football team, Joe's losses to date were $91,000. If the jury found that Notre Dame had committed age discrimination in reckless disregard of the law, they could double it to $182,000. I reserved fifteen minutes to respond to Notre Dame's argument and sat down.

It was a smiling and confident William Hoye who walked up to the podium, and immediately attacked one of my strongest points: if Joe's conduct was so bad, why hadn't anything been said or done about it long ago?

"Mr. Lieberman keeps talking about the fact that Bob didn't criticize Joe while they were on the staff together. The fact is, they were co-workers and friends. There was nothing that Bob Davie could do about Joe Moore's conduct when they were working together. It was only when Bob was elevated to head coach in November of 1996 that he was able to do something about what he knew about Joe Moore's coaching performance and coaching philosophy and coaching style. What did he do? He promptly made the decision—and it was his decision to make. He had the discretion. I don't know how many witnesses you heard testify to that fact. The head coach had the discretion to decide who to hire for his new staff. It wasn't like he waited several years and then fired Joe Moore. Bob Davie didn't have the opportunity until November of 1996 to make a decision concerning Joe Moore, and he made it. He made it based on the merits. He made it based on what he had seen of Joe Moore for three-and-a-half years, and it didn't have anything to do with age.

"By the time Bob became the head coach, he had the opportunity to observe Mr. Moore's job performance, his coaching style, his attitude and his philosophy for three-and-a-half years. It was sort of like a three-and-a-half-year job interview. During that time, Bob Davie came to know that Joe Moore had a physically and verbally abusive coaching style. He had an intimidating coaching philosophy, and he had a disrespectful attitude toward his boss, Lou Holtz.

"So what is the question you have to decide in this case? Simply stated, it's whether Joe Moore and his attorneys proved that Bob Davie intentionally discriminated against Joe Moore on the basis of his age. Did Bob Davie refuse to hire Mr. Moore because of his age or because of the numerous compelling reasons he cited on the witness stand on Friday and on Saturday?

"It's rare for an employer to have an opportunity to decide whether to hire a person they've worked with on a daily basis for more than three years. Bob Davie had that opportunity."

Hoye went over the events at the Florida State 1994 game, and what Phil Lengyel, the Disney executive, told Davie about Moore's conduct. He described the spring 1995 locker room incident: "Folks, these are eighteen-, nineteen- and twenty-year-old kids. Joe Moore was obligated to coach them and to teach them, not to assault them, not to abuse them, and not to humiliate them."

He made a distinction between Davie's permitting two players to settle their personal dispute by going head-to-head in practice wearing helmets and pads, and the way Joe Moore had behaved. "I'm talking about a coach who crossed the line, a coach who abused players, a coach who went down the line, bam, bam, bam, bam, bam." He smashed his fists together for emphasis. "Bob Davie knew everything he needed to know about that incident to make a hiring decision, and it didn't have anything to do with Joe Moore's age. The fact of the matter is that Bob Davie did not want to hire a coach who he knew had physically assaulted the players placed in his charge by Notre Dame. He didn't want to hire an offensive line coach who had abused players."

Hoye asked the jury to do what I had asked them not to do—put themselves in the place of the decision maker.

"Ask yourself, ladies and gentlemen, how could he in good conscience as the new head football coach at Notre Dame in one of his first official acts, hire such a coach? As Notre Dame's new coach, Bob Davie knew that he would have to be the one to explain that decision to the players and their parents if Joe ever should abuse anyone else. There's no way of knowing, when Bob Davie made that decision, whether Joe Moore would assault or abuse or humiliate or intimidate another kid.

"These two hitting incidents standing alone are sufficient to legally justify Bob Davie's decision not to hire Joe Moore.

Although football is a tough sport on the field, that does not make it right or appropriate for coaches to abuse their power by punching and hitting their players in anger off the field. It's unlawful, it's unfair, and it's an abuse of the inherent power coaches have over their players, the power over whether they suit up for a game, the power over whether they play, the power over whether they realize their dreams of playing in the NFL. It's also an abuse of the respect and the admiration that college football players tend to have for their coaches."

Hoye asked the jury to ask themselves if this kind of physical abuse had occurred in an office setting or a warehouse where a supervisor hit a subordinate because he didn't like this performance, "would we even be here?" The answer was obvious: "There is no reason why this conduct should be treated differently just because it involved a football coach and his players."

Hoye also talked about the "mountain of other legitimate non-discriminatory reasons for his decision not to hire Joe Moore"—the incident in the parking lot in Ireland; the punitive use of drills; the verbal abuse and extreme profanity; the absence from mandatory coaches' meetings; disrespectful behavior toward the head coach; smoking in violation of NCAA rules, and declining coaching performance.

As to Davie's desire to maintain continuity with his coaching staff, Hoye told the jury, "Mr. Lieberman argues that continuity is some sort of code word for ageist stereotyping or something. Bob Davie didn't stereotype Joe Moore; he took Joe Moore at his word. As you know—you heard the testimony—Bob Davie learned through repeated conversations with Mr. Moore himself in 1995 and 1996 that Joe only intended to continue coaching for another year, maybe two. As you recall from Coach Davie's testimony, he said that in the December 2nd meeting in Joe's home. Mr. Moore even told Bob that he intended to coach for only another year or two.

"Bob Davie isn't the only person that Joe told that he was only going to coach another year or two. As you'll recall, in 1996 he also told colleagues on the Notre Dame staff, including Charlie Strong and Urban Meyer, that he intended to retire to South Carolina in another year. As you heard him say yesterday, Mr. Moore's statements concerning his retirement plans were not tied to whether Coach Holtz stayed or left Notre Dame. Coach Moore himself admits he was only going to coach three to four more years, in this courtroom.

"Joe Moore was the only assistant coach on the staff who had told Bob Davie and others that he intended to leave. There's a big difference, ladies and gentlemen, between hiring someone for an indefinite foreseeable future on the one hand and hiring a person who has told you and others that he's going to leave in a year or two. The bottom line is Bob didn't want to hire somebody he knew would leave him, especially by a staff that had been plagued by turnover. When you think of continuity, think about Joe Moore telling Bob Davie and his colleagues that he was leaving."

Hoye dismissed my heavy reliance on Davie's mention of Moore's age, accusing me of taking some things out of context and telling only part of the story. Moreover, he pointed out, "merely mentioning somebody's age doesn't

make it age discrimination." Methodically, Hoye dissected
and dismissed each of the alleged age comments: Mosley was
lying because he was angry about being fired; at Moore's
house, the subject of age came up only because Moore
brought it up; each of the players at the December 2nd meeting had a "different recollection of what Bob Davie" said,
whereas "Davie knows exactly what he said, and he explained
it" in the courtroom. Justin Hall's testimony could not be
credited because he looked up to Joe as a friend and mentor,
and "wanted to do everything he could to help Joe Moore.
But even Hall had to admit that Davie was frustrated when
they met because Moore had called Davie a liar, falsely accusing him of telling the players that he had retired. Davie
said, 'Let's face it; he's sixty-four years old,' only in reference to Moore's own statement that he was planning to retire in a year or two. In short," Hoye told the jury, "Bob
Davie's decision had nothing to do with Joe Moore's age
and everything to do with his coaching philosophy, attitude
and style."

And no damages should be awarded, because there was
no discrimination. In any event, the proposed damage calcu-
lations were inaccurate because there was no deduction of
the $39,000 that Moore had received as director of charities
for Tollgrade Communications—that would bring the back
pay amount down to about $35,000. He concluded with an
assurance to the jury that a finding for Notre Dame was the
proper verdict.

Judge Sharp declared a twenty-minute recess. Everyone
left the courtroom; I stayed on alone at the counsel table.
For a trial lawyer, the most frustrating challenge is trying to

divine what is in the jurors' heads. All eight of them had listened attentively to both arguments without giving any indication of their feelings. There were five women on the jury, some of whom must be mothers. Did they disapprove of the brutality in college football? Would they use this case to send a message that Joe's motivational techniques were unacceptable, and Davie's professed kinder and gentler approach was preferable? Would Davie's real reason for getting rid of Joe be lost in Notre Dame's smokescreen defense?

As the jury filed back to their seats, I took three deep breaths, willed myself to expel negative thoughts and stood up to face them. This was not the time to comment once more on the video testimony or talk to the jury as their friend; it was the moment to take control.

"Notre Dame's entire defense is about changing the subject," I said. "The evidence in terms of what motivated Davie at the time of discharge was age, age, age, age. And what do they focus on? They direct your attention to something else." While Notre Dame was trying to divert attention from the question of Joe's age to Joe's conduct, it never answered our questions about its defense. If Davie was really so troubled for so long over Joe's conduct, why didn't he ever talk to anyone about it? When Michael Wadsworth, Father Beauchamp and Kelly interviewed him for the head coaching job, he didn't say a word to them about abuse or anything else, and he never talked to any assistant coaches about it either. He didn't do it even after he was appointed head coach and had the power and authority to discuss any problems he had with Joe.

But what he did do was fire Joe and hire Jim Colletto, even though Colletto had the "same deficiencies that they claim Joe had." Davie never explained in this court why he fired one man for alleged abusive conduct and then immediately hired someone else who exhibited the same deficiencies.

And there was Hoye's point about what would happen at a company if a supervisor struck an employee: "What company do you know fires someone for an infraction that they commit two years after they committed it? Have you ever heard of that? You reprimand an employee and say don't do it again, and it never happens again. Then two years later the employee is fired for that?" Besides, Hoye's comparison of Notre Dame football to a corporation was ludicrous. "This is not a company. This is a big time football team and a big time football program. It is rough and it is tough, and Davie is rough and tough, and Colletto is rough and tough. They're all rough and tough and Davie knows it."

I went over and put my hand on Joe's shoulder. "I said at the beginning of the case that I was proud to represent Joe Moore. The evidence indicates to you where that statement came from. This is a good man and a good coach. He tries his best. He's also a courageous man. He took on Notre Dame because he was wronged. He took them on so maybe the next time they fire somebody, they'll act with some basic level of compassion. They'll think about the laws and not act as if they are somehow above the laws of our country. On behalf of Joe and Mimi and Bill, we ask you to consider the wrong here, and we ask you to right that wrong."

I approached the jury box, standing close to the eight people who would decide the case. "Mr. Davie said, 'Let's face it; he's sixty-four years old.' That is not any different from saying, 'Let's face it; she's a woman,' or 'Let's face it; he's black.'"

We went to wait for the verdict at an old-fashioned, high-ceilinged saloon near the courthouse, where we could get sandwiches. Appropriating three tables in the back of the tavern, we ate and waited. As the hours passed, Joe became increasingly pessimistic. "That farmer on the jury doesn't like me," he muttered. "And those women, I don't like the way some of them reacted. Rick, do we have an appeal if we lose?"

Mimi was almost certain that we had lost. She believed that the long deliberations must mean that the jury was hung up on the abuse questions. At the bar, I confided privately to Rick Mason, "It's ironic. I have spent my career representing management, but from now on I might be known as the lawyer who lost the Joe Moore–Notre Dame case."

As the afternoon dragged on, Fran and I chatted about our families. Fran took out a container of pills, swallowed several and offered some to me. "What are they?" I asked. "St. John's Wort herbal mood elevators," she said. I took three.

Rick Mason told the bartenders and waitresses that we were waiting for a phone call from the court. But the only call from the court came from the bailiff; late in the afternoon he called the tavern to order sandwiches for the jurors. Obviously, they intended to work through dinner. I decided to take a walk. As I started to turn the corner, I heard someone calling me. I stopped and looked back down the street where Rick stood, waving his arms. "The court just called!" he shouted. "The jury has reached a verdict. They must have decided they wanted to go home for dinner."

At the courthouse, we learned the Notre Dame team was still en route from the hotel, twenty minutes away. When

Davie, Wadsworth, Mrs. Wadsworth, the four Notre Dame lawyers and their entourage of technicians and press agents finally arrived, they looked grim. Even Davie looked tense. I hoped that my game face was more relaxed than theirs.

The crowded courtroom was silent; even the cynical reporters seemed on edge. Joe was preparing himself for the worst. Mimi was now positive that the verdict would be for Notre Dame. From a strictly intellectual perspective, I thought that we should win, but viscerally, I was terrified that the jury would rule against us.

The bailiff brought in the jury; they stared straight in front of them, not looking at anyone. Everything seemed to move in slow motion. Judge Sharp said, "This is an important day in the life of these litigants and in the life of this court." He read the verdict to himself impassively, and handed it to the bailiff who gave it to the jury foreperson. I began silently rehearsing what I would say to the press on the courthouse steps if we lost.

The foreperson, the legal secretary, read: "Do you find that the Plaintiff, Joseph R. Moore, has proven by a preponderance of the evidence that he was discharged because of his age?" She paused. "Yes."

I put my hand on Joe's forearm. He showed no emotion, and I wasn't sure he understood. "You won," I whispered.

Mimi blinked back tears.

The foreperson continued: "If you answered question number one 'yes,' then answer this question. Was the conduct of the Defendant willful? Yes."

Then she read the back pay amount: it was $42,935.28, doubled because of the willfulness finding to $85,870.56.

The courtroom remained still as Judge Sharp thanked the jury for their service. Before dismissing them, he said, "I believe deeply there are no winners here." Joe murmured to me, "He must be talking about Notre Dame and himself— not me." As the jurors left the room, one of them—the truck driver—paused, looked at Joe and winked. Joe smiled at him.

When the jury was gone, the judge announced that in accordance with the statute, he was awarding attorneys' fees to Moore's lawyers and instructed us to submit a fee petition. When he asked if there was further business, I collected myself, stood up and said that the plaintiff was also seeking reinstatement to his job or front pay. Judge Sharp's answer was that he would not, under any circumstances, reinstate Moore or provide any further damages.

"Your Honor," I replied, remaining calm, "the statute provides for either reinstatement or front pay for a prevailing party." Perhaps at this point the judge remembered that he had been mistaken about damages under the age law. In any case, he now scheduled a hearing in two weeks to decide the questions of front pay or reinstatement.

As soon as the court adjourned, the reporters rushed to position themselves with the television cameras on the courthouse steps. Our group was the only one left in the courtroom. Weeping, Fran hugged Joe, repeating, "I just can't believe it," over and over again. Slightly dazed, we slowly gathered our belongings. Joe, about to face the media, began to grope for the right words to express his feelings. I had had a statement ready if we lost, but now I had no idea what to say.

We took the small elevator to the first floor and walked across the lobby to the front entrance. Opening the door part way, we were blocked by the back of the massive Michael Wadsworth, standing next to Davie and the rest of the Notre Dame group, facing reporters and cameramen. We waited several minutes for them to move, but Wadsworth seemed to be making a speech. "He'll take the fall for this," Joe said, referring to Wadsworth. There was an adjacent door which I tentatively pushed open. "Let's just go. I'm not waiting for that windbag to finish," Joe said.

As we walked into the late afternoon July sun, the reporters and cameramen deserted Wadsworth in mid-sentence and moved en masse to our group. "How do you feel, Coach Moore?" a reporter asked.

"I'm just grateful the people on the jury believed me," Joe said softly. "People who know me know I don't lie."

"Mr. Lieberman, weren't you disappointed that the jury awarded so little money?"

I felt an unexpected surge of emotion. For the first time since the case started, I spoke without carefully planning a speech in advance—the words just tumbled out. "This was never, ever about the money," I said, and as I spoke, I realized that it was the truth.

AFTERWORD

As the jurors left the courthouse, they refused to talk to the press. But later David Haugh got a scoop: an exclusive interview with the mapmaker juror, who told him what had gone on in the jury room. The eight jurors unanimously decided for Joe within a few minutes, but spent another four-and-a-half hours deciding whether they should deduct Joe's salaries from Tollgrade Communications and the Cathedral Prep High School from the damage recovery—something they finally did.

About Davie, the mapmaker said, "His testimony was inconsistent. Me and the other jurors all thought that. He said he wanted continuity and then he hired people who were inconsistent with that. Continuity was the big word of the trial."

The jurors, he said, did not believe Davie's long list of grievances against Joe: "That his car was not clean was not a good reason to fire him." In contrast to their hostility to Davie, the jurors felt Joe was "one of them." None of the jurors, including the five mothers on the panel, believed that Notre Dame fired Joe for abusing players. "We talked about it, but we pretty well figured that these were football players who get hit a lot anyway, you know, young adults. Even in their testimony, one of them said he looked at [Joe slapping him] as more of a joke. It couldn't have been that bad."

Several months after the verdict, Judge Sharp awarded Joe additional damages—two years of front pay, less his salary at his current jobs, for a total of $75,600. The judge ruled that Joe was entitled to this award because he had not been fully compensated by the jury's back pay award; they had not taken into account his having been deprived by Notre Dame of future benefits, salary and the prestige of his line of work. And Joe's near-retirement age meant he "would have no reasonable prospect of finding a comparable position." The judge also awarded attorneys' fees and expenses of $394,865 to our legal team—although our actual fees (based on number of hours worked times hourly rates) and expenses came to $625,000.

We appealed Judge Sharp's dismissal of Joe's defamation claim as well as the award for attorneys' fees. The appeal was settled in December 1998 when Notre Dame agreed to pay another $85,000.

In the aftermath of the trial, Notre Dame took a beating in the press. The headlines said it all: *USA Today*: "Damage to Notre Dame Far More than Amount Awarded in Lawsuit"; the *New York Times*: "Teetering on Its Pedestal/Notre Dame's Reputation is Marred by Off-the-Field Troubles"; editorial in the *Chicago Tribune*: "A Big Loss for the Fighting Irish"; *Sports Illustrated*: "Flagged Before the Play"; the *Washington Post*: "Days of Reckoning/Notre Dame's Revelations aren't College Football's." *The Sporting News* suggested that "to save its pristine reputation, Notre Dame should suspend football just as any institute would suspend an unruly fraternity."

Notre Dame had to hope that the bad publicity would abate within a short time, but it did not. In the fall, a short documentary on the case was shown on ESPN. Even NBC, the network that paid millions to Notre Dame for national broadcasting rights, criticized the university on a national broadcast for not settling the case.

Concerned that the stain on its reputation would affect donations, the Notre Dame Annual Fund sent a letter to its vast alumni population, saying: "Let's face it. Notre Dame has taken it on the chin the past couple of months and I fear that some of us doubt if Notre Dame is heroic anymore. I ask you to have faith."

Notre Dame alumni and faculty undoubtedly kept their faith in the institution, but their confidence in the administration was shaken. Five months after the trial, Notre Dame's faculty senate asked the university president Edward Malloy whether there was any truth to "persistent reports" that the decision to go forward with the Moore lawsuit had been made against the advice of lawyers both inside and outside the university.

A Notre Dame Theology professor wrote President Malloy, "There are faculty who are concerned about the harm that was done to the university by the case. They are concerned about whether someone, contrary to legal advice, put the reputation of the university at risk. These reports are discussed and circulated, and people are interested in knowing whether they are true." President Malloy declined to provide further information. Father Beauchamp refused to meet with the faculty senate to explain the handling of the case.

Several members of the university's powerful board of trustees were strongly critical of the decision to fight Joe Moore.

The administration continued to support Bob Davie, who, possibly in an attempt to avoid further controversy, behaved so cautiously that he seemed dull and pessimistic. The fans, used to larger-than-life coaches, were less than enthusiastic about Davie. Even his 9-3 record for the 1998–99 season was considered mediocre, and he was blamed for an injury suffered by his star quarterback when Davie put him in a vulnerable position in an attempt to take a game-ending safety. The next season, Davie won only five of twelve games and, for the first time in its history, Notre Dame football received an NCAA probation, based in large part on the acceptance of improper gifts from a fan who had lavished presents and vacation trips on players with embezzled money.

The loyal alumni had had enough. Twenty influential graduates sent a letter to the board of trustees complaining about mismanagement of the athletic department, with a focus on the Joe Moore and NCAA fiascos. Michael Wadsworth wrote a letter in his own defense to the alumni, but it was too little, too late. In February, 2000, Wadsworth was fired and all responsibilities for the athletic department were taken from Father Beauchamp, who resigned his executive vice presidency several months later.

In the months following the trial, Joe received congratulatory calls from over a dozen former Notre Dame football players, as well as from coaches and friends. When he reported to the Baltimore Ravens training camp a week after the trial, virtually every coach told him he had done the right thing.

Joe and Fran settled in Erie, Pennsylvania, near their family. Joe continued to work with the Baltimore Ravens, to plan charitable events for Tollgrade, and to coach the football team at Cathedral Prep, his grandson's high school. This was a program that had been mediocre for years; under Joe's guidance the team reached the Pennsylvania semifinals in the 1998 season.

When an AP reporter, preparing a personality profile, asked him why he was doing a job for which he was overqualified, Joe said, "It's not all that different . . . it's football, it's teaching, it's fundamentals, and it's basic things. I was going to do something in football this year and next year and the year after. I just want to make sure I'm enjoying it." About the trial, he said, "They used all the power they had to destroy me as a person. But I'll never quit loving Notre Dame. I don't know if anybody who ever coached there had as strong feelings as I did."

Joe spent most of his time at Cathedral Prep coaching the defense, leaving the offensive line coaching to Rick Kaczenski, one of the Notre Dame players who was in the locker room at halftime in spring 1995. When they weren't coaching, Joe helped train Kaczenski for tryouts with the NFL.

In December 1998, two years after Joe was fired, he turned down the offensive line coaching job at Iowa State, because, he said, he preferred amateur sports. Later, Lou Holtz, now head coach at the University of South Carolina, offered Joe the offensive line coaching job there. Joe politely declined.

When Notre Dame's 1999 season started, it was widely believed that Davie would be fired at the end of the season.

But when the team ended the season with a 9-2 record and an invitation to play in the Fiesta Bowl, Notre Dame extended Davie's contract through 2005. Explaining the rationale for this extension, the university's Athletic Director Kevin White said, "Plus, and this is as important as any of his achievements, Bob embraces the principles and values Notre Dame represents."

In the wake of the Moore case, it is unlikely that any college or professional sports organization will make an employment decision about an older coach without considering the age discrimination ramifications. And it's a good bet that the real legacy of the case will be many more coaches still working in their sixties and seventies. This is for the best: coaches with experience and wisdom have a great deal to contribute. If that is the legacy of Joe Moore's case, he will be very happy.

SOURCES & ACKNOWLEDGMENTS

The book is based on the court and deposition records of the case, Ross & Hardies' internal case files, formal and informal interviews of participants, and newspaper and television accounts of the case.* Obviously, the story is told primarily from the Moores' perspective. The University of Notre Dame may well have a different perspective, and I hope they share it in some subsequent account of the case.

I would not have started or finished this book without the encouragement and forbearance of my wife, Tina, who put up with my mental absence from family life while I was working on it. Mimi Moore, my colleague, not only encouraged me to pursue this project but spent many hours reviewing the drafts for accuracy and completeness. Vi Michalczyk, my assistant, was invaluable, not only for her patience in typing and retyping the manuscript, but for her editorial service. My friend Tom Leavens also contributed editorial advice, encouragement and an introduction to my publisher, Academy Chicago. The editorial work of Dr. Anita Miller of Academy Chicago was both astute and meticulous resulting in a markedly improved manuscript. I also thank Jordan Miller for his insight and hard work. In addition, my sister

Barbara Lieberman, Paul Rozmarek and Gary Smith made significant contributions to the project. My most profound thanks go to the Moores for trusting me with their case and their story.

*Quotations from the deposition and court transcripts have, in some instances, been slightly edited for reasons of grammatical correctness, punctuation or clarity; there has been no attempt to color the testimony.

INDEX